PRODUCTIVE AGING

ROBERT N. BUTLER, M.D., is Brookdale Professor of Geriatrics and Adult Development at Mount Sinai School of Medicine in New York City, as well as Chairman of that school's Gerald and May Ellen Ritter Department of Geriatrics and Adult Development. He also is Meritorious Professor of Gerontology and Geriatrics at Hunter College in New York City. He formerly served as the first director of the National Institute on Aging, one of 11 institutes of the National Institutes of Health, the main biomedical research agency of the U.S. government. Dr. Butler is the author of a number of books, including *Why Survive? Being Old in America,* which won a Pulitzer Prize in 1976; *Human Aging* (co-author); *Aging and Mental Health* (co-author); *Sex After Sixty* (co-author); and *Love and Sex After Sixty.* He has published some 200 research and clinical papers in the fields of cerebral physiology, life cycle, middle age and aging, psychotherapy, confidentiality, drugs, and creativity. In addition, Dr. Butler writes book reviews and articles regularly for newspapers and magazines. He is on the editorial board of several journals, including *Age and Aging Journal, Geriatrics, International Journal of Aging and Human Development, Journal of Geriatric Psychiatry,* and *Journal of Neurobiology of Aging: Experimental and Clinical Research.* He has taught at Howard and George Washington Universities.

HERBERT P. GLEASON is Legal Counsel to the Boston Health Plan, a health maintenance organization whose members use Boston Neighborhood Health Centers as their primary care providers. He is a Director of the Health Planning Council of Greater Boston and a Trustee of the Brigham and Women's Hospital. Mr. Gleason served as Corporation Counsel and Chairman of the Board of Health and Hospitals of the City of Boston. He is Acting President and Secretary of the Salzburg Seminar, where he has taught at two other sessions in the area of health. Mr. Gleason has edited a book (*Getting Better*) summarizing the 1979 session at Salzburg, as well as a survey of Boston's Neighborhood Health Centers (*A Promise Kept*).

PRODUCTIVE AGING
Enhancing Vitality in Later Life

Robert N. Butler, M.D.
Herbert P. Gleason

Editors

SPRINGER PUBLISHING COMPANY
New York

Springer Publishing Company, Inc.
536 Broadway
New York, New York 10012

85 86 87 88 89 / 10 9 8 7 6 5 4 3 2 1

Library of Congress Cataloging-in-Publication Data

Main entry under title:

Productive aging.
   Includes bibliographies and index.
   1. Aged—Congresses. 2. Life span, Productive—Congresses. 3. Ability, Influence of age on—Congresses. 4. Aged—Employment—Congresses. 5. Old age assistance—United States—Congresses. I. Butler, Robert N. II. Gleason, Herbert P.
HQ1061.P78 1985   305.2'6   85-14790
ISBN 0-8261-4810-7

Printed in the United States of America

Contents

The Salzburg Seminar

The Salzburg Seminar is a private, independent, nonprofit educational organization established in 1947 by Harvard University students for the purpose of bringing together promising young European intellectuals with prominent American scholars in order to learn about American society. Since that time, the purpose of the Seminar has broadened to include the study of contemporary problems with a world-wide scope. The Seminar provides a unique forum for the frank exchange of ideas and informed opinion. While offering fellows from the Middle East, Africa, and Europe insights into developments in the United States, it familiarizes American participants with ideas and attitudes of other countries.

Every year the Seminar offers approximately ten sessions, each lasting from one to three weeks. Each session has a different subject, faculty, and group of fellows. Approximately fifty men and women participate at one time. They are chosen to reflect a diversity of professional viewpoints and experiences. Most fellows are in their thirties, though some are younger, some older. They work with a distinguished international faculty, all of whom serve without compensation.

Presently, there are nearly 12,000 alumni of the Salzburg Seminar, including current and former prime ministers; members of parliaments and cabinets; ambassadors; mayors of major cities; and leaders in the arts, business, education, and the legal and medical professions.

Preface

In his introduction to this book, Robert Butler describes his meeting with David Hamburg, Maurice Lazarus, and me to plan a session on aging to take place in 1983 at the Salzburg Seminar. It had been my conception, after our general session on health in Salzburg in 1979, that the session on aging should be devoted to planning better care for the elderly. In Salzburg in 1979, Sir George Godber had enlisted all of us in the cause of enabling the elderly to continue functioning independently. From him we knew that "the ideal situation for elderly people is continued independent living in their own homes," that "self-reliance is the best emotional, and, therefore, somatic condition," that "it is a grave error to think of the health and welfare needs of the elderly as being mainly for long-term care in hospitals or nursing homes" (Gleason, 1980). In the 1983 session I wanted to develop ways of achieving those goals.

When we first met, Robert Butler announced that if he were going to chair it, the session would be called "Health, Productivity, and Aging." I suggested that "Activity" would be more comprehensive and generally understood, but Butler was adamant. So I acquiesced, and during the next few months of fund raising and fellow selection, we were constantly explaining that the session was not about old people in industry.

Even when 50 of us assembled in Salzburg, discussion dwelt on the management of nursing homes, reimbursement decisions, and pension policy. But Butler had chosen his faculty with care. James Birren, Betty Friedan, and Alvar Svanborg were all indoctrinated. Each had already realized that productivity was the catalyst that would clarify every solution for older people. Whether for pay or not, in traditional roles or not, productive activity sustains their psychological, social, and, in some cases, economic freedom. It maintains vigorous lifestyles and thus alters the public image of the elderly as frail and dependent. It forces society to scrutinize employment, retirement, and pension policies. The participation of older people enriches societies economically, culturally, and spiritually.

This book is a testament to the clarifying and unifying function of Butler's idea. All of its chapters are shaped by the fellows' response to it. Their contributions cannot be presented adequately here, but their sense is set forth in the "Common Themes" and "Process" sections that appear as appendices at the end of this book.

The authors do not sing in unison, but, without editorial compulsion, they are harmonious. Whether the insights come from James Birren's tender attention to the psyche, Betty Friedan's lessons from women's liberation, Maurice Lazarus' experience in the marketplace, or Alvar Svanborg's patient measurement of physique, age begins to make sense.

I could not begin to thank all the people whose assistance was essential to bringing this session about. Special thanks go to Sir George Godber, James Fries of Stanford University, and Alexander Leaf of the Massachusetts General Hospital. The session and this book could not have happened without substantial support from the Pew Memorial Trust. The Henry J. Kaiser Foundation also contributed generously.

John Tuthill has long accepted the message of this book. In his eight years as president of the Salzburg Seminar, he has engaged the productive capacities of countless directors and friends in responsible tasks. By doing so, he has enriched them and the institution. The Salzburg Seminar would not exist without the wisdom and experience of Roger Lort, who has served it in every capacity for 18 years. His well-modulated reminders of neglected duties kept the project and me in motion.

I am indebted to Karyn Donovan, Annie Thomas, and Adriane Rothstein for their patient retypings of the manuscript.

Herbert P. Gleason

REFERENCES

Gleason, H. (Ed.) (1980). *Getting better, A report on health care from the Salzburg Seminar*. Cambridge, Mass.: Oelgeschlager, Gunn, & Hain.

Introduction

In the spring of 1981, David Hamburg, excited by his experience at the 1979 health session at the Salzburg Seminar, asked if I would participate in the first program on aging to be held at Salzburg. Later, he arranged for me to meet with him, Herbert Gleason, and Maurice Lazarus. They asked me to chair the faculty and select the topic.

For the topic, I urged that we move away from the popular concepts of dependency, long-term care, and costs of old age (all admittedly important) to a largely undeveloped topic, that of productivity in old age.

Fortunately, I was able to entice two renowned scientists to join us: Alvar Svanborg from Gothenburg, Sweden, a world authority on the good physiological news about aging; and James Birren from Los Angeles, whose research on psychological growth with age is demolishing the cliché, "You seem so young!" Maurice Lazarus helped me persuade Betty Friedan to come and infuse our discussions about productive aging with the energy released by the women's movement in the United States.

I regard productive aging as a critical subject, emerging as a powerful political issue. It is also an old interest of mine. In 1974 when writing *Why Survive? Being Old in America,* I almost decided to eliminate a chapter on "the right to work." I was afraid it was too radical and would weaken the public's reception of the entire work. Yet since that time there have been great strides in legislative efforts to reduce employment discrimination on the basis of old age. For example, mandatory retirement has been raised to 70 in the private sector. In 1979, I pressed our research planning group at the National Institute on Aging to emphasize the issue of productivity in old age.

My own long-standing interest in the relationships among aging, productivity, and health was reinforced in no small measure by experiences gained during travels to different countries, Japan and the

Soviet Union among them. I certainly was struck in Japan, the third most productive nation of the world, by uneasiness about the "graying of Japan." It is the fastest aging nation in the world; in the year 2010, some 20 percent of its population will be over 65 years of age. The "raw materials" of Japan are not physical resources or energy, but human resources. Japanese workers are involved to a very considerable extent in high technology. Some Japanese policy makers and managers are concerned with the impact of an aging society upon productivity. In the Soviet Union, where approximately 20 million men died in World War II, there are worker shortages. There, gerontology has been conducted at the factory level; that is, efforts are made to alter the work conditions and work tasks to take into account the residual capacities of persons as they grow older.

How do we orient our attention toward productivity rather than dependency? For example, we might very well have entitled the three-week seminar in Salzburg, "Dependency and Aging." Many people express concern about the costs and dependency of old age. But we wanted to look at aging from a more positive point of view. I wanted to stress the mobilization of the productive potential of the elders of society. At Salzburg we asked, How can older people continue to work, to participate, to volunteer, to maintain and promote their own health and self-care, to accept responsibility for being in the vanguard of socioeconomic and cultural change? In other words, can older persons themselves be pioneers in this century of old age?

Health and productivity are interesting conditions: The unproductive person who is divided from the social role of work is at higher risk of illness as well as economic dependency; and the sick person is limited in productivity and, therefore, at higher risk of dependency. Very often, health and productivity go hand in hand and deteriorate together, whether the first loss is in one realm or the other. Moreover, social reaction to sickness and lack of productivity may raise the pressures on the dependent—they may be ignored, dismissed, and undersupported. We even have laws to forbid productivity (e.g., the limit on Social Security benefits for earners), and we set up labor and fringe-benefit conditions to make it hard for older workers to keep and return to jobs if they retire.

Of course, productivity will not solve all the income and care needs of older people. So we must ask, What does society owe its elders for having provided the infrastructure, the capital base, the care and education of children and grandchildren? In terms of equity, should older people share in any rising standard of living? Should they in fact receive more? The ethical question arises if special consideration should be given to older persons. Should there be a late-life dividend for a lifetime investment in a particular society? What resources is society prepared to make available to its elderly members? How prepared are other groups and interests in society to accept the moral claim of the elders? Is there the possibility of scapegoating? Is there a possibility of blame being placed on older persons because of their claim upon society's resources? What are the other claims for society's resources—housing, the military, recreation, transportation, and so forth? How do we set priorities? How should the growth in a particular society be spent?

At Salzburg, I wanted to focus on what I have called the triumph of survivorship—the worldwide graying or aging of nations and the paradoxical fact that there appear to be very few people who are celebrating this unprecedented achievement of increased life expectancy. Worse yet, there are gloomy predictions from many parts of the world that we are on a "collision course" between resources and the claims of old age. I think the contemporary economic framework shapes our discussion unduly. The era of abundance in some societies is being replaced by a kind of politics or rhetoric of austerity that is reinforced by the reality of worldwide economic pertubations. Certain groups and ideologies are exploiting economic realities. Demography is significant: There is an extraordinary change in age composition. But demography per se is not the driving force of current or even of future economic distress. Other forces of far greater influence are at work. Moreover, it is not prudent to make certain commitments affecting old age in the next century, as if present economic considerations will remain operative. Nonetheless, there are reasons for examining the interrelationships among aging, health, and productivity, reasons that will be, and are, advantageous to contemporary societies and to individual older persons, now and in the future.

After endeavoring to arrive at definitions of our categories—aging, health, and productivity—we developed in Salzburg an action agenda designed to shatter contemporary stereotypes and sharpen the focus with regard to the moral, ethical, economic, and cultural issues affecting the support of a nation's elderly. The graying of society, population aging, while a remarkable achievement indeed, is not really quite so extraordinary as is sometimes said. We can and undoubtedly will experience, with standard biomedical research and with the possibilities of life-extension research, far higher numbers and relative proportions of older persons, with greatly prolonged life expectancy, achieved simultaneously with reductions of morbidity and debility. We can and will absorb the aged into our productivity and reshape the very concepts of what we mean by the "productive base" of our society. The maturation of society can be preferable to some of the negative aspects of youth-dominated societies such as unemployment, violence, impetuosity, and crime.

Some of our feelings related to health and productivity have been present throughout history. The following is a quote from the American social scientist, William Graham Sumner, in *Folkways*, published in 1907:

> [There are] two sets of mores as to the aged: 1) in one set of mores the teaching, and usages, inculcate conventional respect for the aged who are therefore arbitrarily preserved for their wisdom and counsel, perhaps also sometimes out of affection and sympathy [notice only sometimes] . . . 2) in the other set of mores the aged are regarded as societal burdens [this is 1907] . . . which waste the strength of the society, already inadequate for its tasks. Therefore, they are forced to die, either by their own hands or those of their relatives. It is very far from being true that the first of these policies is practiced higher up in civilization than those who practice the second. The people in lower civilizations profit more by the counsel from the aged than those in higher civilizations and are educated by this experience to respect and value the aged.

As it turned out, the fellows who attended the session on health, productivity, and aging at Salzburg were about evenly divided among America, Europe, the Near East, and Africa. As a result, our discussions about how developed countries could better use the capacities of older people were enriched by descriptions of societies that still do.

Without leaving home, the reader will join our Seminar on an intellectual odyssey and find, I hope, that the final page brings one back home—a home that is somehow different because of new perceptions and values.

My overview (Chapter 1) shows the barriers to incentive and

opportunity that deprive our older selves, individually and collectively, of material, intellectual, and spiritual wealth. Because of deeply-rooted negativism about old age and aging in our culture, many people ignore the triumph of survival into their 80s and 90s. This ageism springs from fears of becoming economically and physically dependent, and from ignorance about the scientific process of aging. Much can be done by overcoming the barriers, realizing the productive potential in paid, altruistic, or other activity, and by protecting against social isolation and ruinous expenses of long-term care. The triumph of age is also a challenge.

In Chapter 2, Alvar Svanborg presents some good news: how more recent cohorts of Swedish 70-year-olds are healthier and more able than their predecessors. While the risk of falling ill does increase in old age, more years of relative health have been added to average life expectancy. The human being is a remarkably sturdy and healthy creature. Homo sapiens has the capacity to guard against accidents and the complications of illness. The chances of survival into advanced age are or can be raised by adaptation of behavior to physical and social environments. This includes timely health and social services, personal action against alcohol abuse and cigaret smoking habits, and institutional changes to minimize social isolation and inactivity. The last group includes creating housing arrangements, barrier free inside and outside environments, and social supportive networks that are tools for counteracting or compensating for losses of function in older persons. Thus, a biomedical scientist and clinician identifies not only the medical, but also the psychosocial instruments with which improved longevity and quality of life may be achieved.

The persistence of competence during a long life is a prime focus of James Birren in Chapter 3. Assumptions about the incapacity of older people are unsound. He reminds us of the great diversity of the later-life population in terms of biological, social, and psychological status. If we open our eyes, we will see that old people have rich adaptive capacities to meet changes in their lives and environments. Their capacities and experiences are a source of wisdom useful to the young. Birren gives us a sense of the developmental mosaic of aging: While becoming more vulnerable to disease, the individual may generate new roles, develop new concepts and perceptions of self and society, and take up new careers and vocations. Disease, more than age, plays the dramatic limiting role in the ability to function and make compensations. The performance of the brain is an example. The normal brain remains active throughout life, but the diseased brain loses information. Birren's outlook implies that aging at the social and psychological levels is highly malleable. Genetic determinism is far from the whole story of aging. (The wisdom of the elderly is knowing how to operate within limitations.)

From her experience in the women's liberation movement, Betty Friedan (Chapter 4) sees ageism as a counterpart in oppressiveness to the feminine mystique. Stereotyping people by age is as damaging as by sex. The complex reality of being a person must be understood. She presents her own struggles as a woman and an aging person to overcome hobbling self-concepts and group prejudices. Problems of an old-age population are principally the problems of women because they outlive men, though men tend to dominate the definition of issues and solutions. This differential in life expectancy is worrisome for women; it raises questions for both sexes. If men are stuck in dull routines, this affects the quality of women's lives, too. Friedan reminds us that the next stage of the women's movement will deal with men's problems and the need for social reconstruction. Both sexes have an interest in replacing the dreary image of age with the vital reality of older men and women. Opportunities for and encouragement of individuality in productive behavior should be a cornerstone of policy-making for an aging population.

The meaning of work to older people and their labor force participation)are considered by Maurice Lazarus and Harvey Lauer (Chapter 5), mainly in the United States. In a society emphasizing the work ethic and conferring social and personal identity primarily through the work role, what is the meaning of the heavy exodus from paid employment in the seventh decade of life? Are pension programs that good? Are jobs that bad? As average life expectancy rises and more wealth is needed for the additional years, aren't people motivated to continue working? Lazarus and Lauer pick up an echo of the earlier chapters when they comment: "The increase in life expectancy and good health is of little benefit to people who are denied the self-esteem and fulfillment derived from satisfying and meaningful activities," such as institutionalized work. In the preretirement years, many people say they would like to continue working, more for psychological than financial reasons in many instances. Actually, only 1 in 8 older persons remains in the workforce after age 65. The authors consider various approaches to raising the proportion: flexibility in hours, an understanding of physical limitations, freedom from age prejudice in management, and removal of penalties in pension and Social Security programs. None of these will happen where employers persist in believing myths about the inferior qualities of older workers. "In most jobs, a worker's capacity to perform far exceeds the demands of the job," the authors say. This chapter should be useful not only to personnel managers and older workers, but to corporate and government policymakers in societies with large health care expenses. By providing encouragement and opportunities for productive behavior in paid and other activities, employers may minimize the potential costs to us all of depressed, diseased, and dependent citizens. Indeed, if the entire workspan is examined for consequences to well-being in old age, benefits might accrue to young and old. One may argue that the humanization of work is socially and corporately prudent.

I will let the dialogue between Betty Friedan and Maurice Lazarus on "Opportunities" (Chapter 6) speak for itself, except to emphasize one point. No one at the seminar argued for make-work projects for the elderly. This kind of opportunity is counterproductive; it trivializes the elderly. They are a precious resource for meeting many societal needs in the public and private sectors—regardless of functional problems. A handicap need not preclude productivity. Rather, disability should be viewed as the net result of an individual-environment equation. An obstructive environment magnifies an individual's problem; an assistive environment promotes productivity. Friedan and Lazarus agree that the opportunity to be productive is an issue for society as a whole, not just its manufacturing and service institutions.

In Chapter 7, Svanborg urges us to find a balanced view between unrealistic positive and negative concepts of aging and the aged. Of particular note is his statement that "activity . . . often has therapeutic and prophylactic effect. Use of productive ability of the elderly not only would tap wasted resources but also would prevent and postpone disability." (Consider the problems of calcium loss shared by astronauts in space and nursing home patients confined to bed.) This notion sets the stage for intervention strategies: not only to eliminate environmental and attitudinal barriers, but also to structure environments and expectations to promote such behavior, minimize dependence, and foster health. The elderly, especially after age 75, need early and correct diagnosis and treatment measures to prevent and postpone sickness and accidents; this implies comprehensive health and social services. At the same time, steps need to be taken to eliminate or reduce barriers to social interaction and productive behavior in housing projects, thoroughfares, public transportation, and employment.

In Chapter 8 on "Changing Sex Roles: Vital Aging," Friedan considers "sense of control over one's life" as a health factor. She believes the improvement of women's health in the 1954–1974 period was partly a result of the new sense of self and treatment of women fostered by the women's liberation movement. Men's health status did not improve in this period, according to data available to Friedan. Why this difference? She speculates that men tend to specialize in instrumental roles in which few achieve control of their lives. Women are more likely to define their own identities and achieve a sense of control. They tend to be more open to change as their roles vary through life. She believes that stereotyping people into confining roles is as harmful when based on sex as when based on age. The contemporary task lies in breaking the false images to liberate productive and fulfilling behavior.

Institutional maladaptation in the United States is exemplified in Chapter 9. Herbert Gleason tells us that Medicare is out of phase with many needs of the elderly. The emphasis on acute care and proscription of long-term or custodial care and preventive services are clues to the origin of Medicare in political compromises. These ignored important geriatric realities. What would Medicare look like if suited to geriatrics? We get some notion in recent Medicare developments of how to facilitate the use of health maintenance organizations: by combining prepaid group medical practice and hospital services under a common budget. Savings through this approach allow extra benefits to be added to the Medicare list. The addition of social supportive services to Medicare would be one step toward creating a base for comprehensive geriatric care. Another would be providing counseling for people who need to find outlets for their productive capacities and ways to overcome social isolation.

The worldwide nature of many issues touched on in earlier chapters is summarized by Judith Howe in Chapter 10, "The United Nations World Assembly on Aging." This is partly the story of how different nations attempt to define the problems and circumstances of their own aging population. In most of the lesser-developed world, older people's special needs remain low national priorities. The Assembly sought to establish a useful international knowledge base to deal with erosion of traditional family arrangements (because of industrialization and urbanization), intergenerational strains, and inadequate services and social supports for older people. An international plan of action on aging, prepared by the Assembly, will be evaluated from time to time.

The process by which the Salzburg Seminar came to grips with personal and social issues of aging is recalled by Friedan in a postscript (and documented in an appendix by Mal Schechter). When confronted by issues on various levels, the Seminar showed that people of various cultures can break old images. This triumph of spirit and intellect is a necessary correlate of the triumph of age. There is hope that group and societal collaborations will develop ideas, knowledge, and consensuses for action.

Robert N. Butler

Faculty, Rapporteurs, and Fellows

FACULTY

JAMES E. BIRREN, who lives in Los Angeles, is Executive Director of the Ethel Percy Andrus Gerontology Center and is Dean of the Leonard Davis School of Gerontology at the University of Southern California. Professor Birren's long and active experience in the field of aging has included service as President of the Gerontological Society (1961–1962), Editor-in-Chief of the *Journal of Gerontology* (1968–1974), and research psychologist at the Institute of Mental Health, the National Heart Institute, and several other institutions. He is, or has been, a leader of a number of special groups or commissions, including the White House Conference on Aging, the Aging Review Committee of the National Institute of Aging, the Steering Committee for Care of the Elderly at the Institute of Medicine, and the National Advisory Committee of the Work in America Institute. Professor Birren was educated at Chicago State University, Northwestern University, and the University of Chicago. He was a visiting scientist at Cambridge University, and he taught for a number of years at the University of Chicago before joining the University of Southern California. Professor Birren's many awards include the Gerontological Society Award for Meritorious Research and the American Pioneers in Aging Award from the University of Michigan.

BETTY FRIEDAN resides in New York City. Her academic assignments have included visiting professorships at the New School of Social Research, Temple University, Yale University, Queen's College, and a Fellowship at the Kennedy School of Government's Institute for Politics at Harvard University. From 1979 to 1981 she was a senior research associate at the Center for the Social Sciences of

Columbia University, where she did research on changing sex roles and the aging process under grants from the Ford Foundation and the National Endowment for the Humanities. Ms. Friedan was a founder and the first president (1966–1970) of the National Organization for Women. She organized the Women's Strike for Equality in 1970 and convened the 1971 National Women's Political Caucus. She was a contributing editor of *McCalls* magazine and currently is on the editorial board of *Present Tense* magazine. Her articles appear in a large number of journals and magazines. She has published three books: *The Feminine Mystique, It Changed My Life,* and *The Second Stage.* She won the Author of the Year Award of the American Society of Journalists and Authors in 1982, and its Humanist of the Year Award in 1975. Ms. Friedan was educated at Smith College and the University of California at Berkeley.

MAURICE LAZARUS lives in Cambridge, Massachussetts and is a Director and Chairman of the Executive Committee of the Harvard Community Health Plan. He is a member of the Visiting Committee to the Harvard School of Public Health; of the Advisory Committee, American Hospital Association/Robert Wood Johnson Foundation Program for Hospital Initiatives in Long Term Care; a Trustee of the Massachussetts General Hospital; and Chairman of the Executive Committee of the Public Agenda Foundation. He is a graduate of Harvard College.

ALVAR SVANBORG, a resident of Gothenburg, Sweden, is Professor of Geriatric and Long Term Medicine at the University of Gothenberg. He has been President of the Federation of Gerontology of the Nordic Countries since 1973 and an advisor/consultant to the World Health Organization since 1970. Professor Svanborg is a member of the National Advisory Board of Sweden and also serves as an advisor to the U.S. Government. He was a member of the Swedish Delegation to the United Nations World Assembly on Aging in 1982. He became Physician-in-Chief of the Vasa Hospital Geriatric Clinic in 1966 and served as Chairman of the Vasa Hospital from 1968 to 1977. Professor Svanborg has published some 350 articles in medical biochemistry, clinical physiology, internal medicine, medical gerontology, and geriatric and long-term care medicine. He was educated at the Karolinska Institute in Stockholm, from which he received his doctorate degree.

RAPPORTEURS

JUDITH L. HOWE lives in New York City and is Administrator of the Department of Geriatrics and Adult Development at the Mount Sinai Medical Center, New York. She has served as an advisor for the United Nations World Assembly on Aging (1982) and as a staff member of the National Institute on Aging, U.S. Department of Health and Human Services (1977–1982). Ms. Howe is a graduate of St. Lawrence University and received an M.P.A. from Syracuse University.

HARVEY LAUER was Senior Research Analyst at the Public Agenda Foundation. He directed the United States Survey Research effort for a six-country study titled "Jobs in the 1980s and 1990s" which provided primary data for his chapter included in this volume. He holds a Master's degree in Psychology from the New School for Social Research in New York City.

MAL SCHECHTER is a resident of New York City and is Senior Teaching Associate and Associate Director of the Center for Productive Aging at the Mount Sinai Medical Center's Ritter Department of Geriatrics and Human Development, New York. Mr. Schechter is a graduate of Columbia University School of Journalism.

FELLOWS

MARIE-JOSEPHINE AARTS-POSTMES, who lives in Nijmegen, Holland, is a psychologist at the Scholengemeenschap Nijmegen-Oost and a lecturer in psychology at Opleidingen, Bejaardenwerk, Utrecht, and Volksuniversiteit, Nijmegen. She graduated with a degree in Educational Psychology from the University of Utrecht.

EMAD ABDEL-KADER lives in Cairo, Egypt, and is a resident physician at Aluminum Company Hospital. Currently he is on service with Offshore International S.A. in the Red Sea. He holds an M.B. and B.Ch. from Ain Shams University, Cairo and is preparing for his Master's degree in General Medicine.

HAIFA AL-BASHIR, of Amman, Jordan, is a member of the National Consultative Council, the National Health Board, and the Jordan

Women's Society and is founder and President of the "Ladies of the White Beds Society," a charity organization for the sick and the aged. She is a graduate in Nursing and Teaching from Jordan University.

OLFAT ALI, of Cairo, Egypt, is a professor and Head of the Department of Public Health and Preventive Medicine at Mansoura University, Egypt. She holds a Ph.D. from the London School of Hygiene and Tropical Medicine and graduated with a degree in Medicine from Ain Shams University, Cairo.

GARY ANDREWS, from Westmeed, Australia, is a professor of community and geriatric medicine at the University of Sydney; a former Director of Health of Australia's Western Metropolitan Health Region; and is Commissioner of the Health Commission of New South Wales. He holds M.B. and B.S. degrees from the University of Sydney.

LINDA BERGLIN lives in St. Paul, Minnesota, and is a state senator, chairing the Committee for Health and Human Services. She is the first woman to serve as a full committee chair of the Minnesota State Senate. She is a founding member of the Education Exploration Center and Better Jobs for Women, and holds a B.F.A. from Minneapolis College of Art and Design.

MARIA HELENA BERNARDO, a resident of Lisbon, Portugal, is Coordinator of the Department for the Elderly and the Handicapped, Ministry of Social Affairs. She holds a B.S. in Educational Nursing from the University of Montreal and a Master's degree in Social Sciences from the Universidade Technica de Lisboa. She participated in the Council of International Programs' study of the aged in Minneapolis and St. Paul, Minnesota.

NACER CHRAIBI lives in Casablanca, Morocco, and is a professor of cardiology in the Department of Medicine at the University of Casablanca. He is a member of the Moroccan and French Society of Cardiology and the Moroccan Association for the Prevention of Heart Diseases. He graduated with degrees in General Medicine and Cardiology from the universities of Rabat, Nancy, Strasbourg, and Paris.

JIM FLYNN, of Newry, Northern Ireland, is a social worker responsible for services to the elderly provided by the Southern Health and

Social Services Board, Newry, Northern Ireland. He is a graduate in Social Work from Leeds Polytechnic and is a trade unionist and member of the local Trade Union Council.

ISTVAN GERGELY, a resident of Budapest, Hungary, is a research associate at Semmelweis Medical University Gerontology Center, Budapest. He earned his M.D. at Semmelweis Medical University where he received his Certificate in Internal Medicine in 1977. He has conducted research into the U.S. system of social and medical care for the aged, done at Syracuse University in 1982.

NANCY A. GLEASON lives in Boston, Massachusetts, and is a social worker in the Stone Center for Developmental Services and Studies at Wellesley College, the Brookline Visiting Nurses, and in private practice. She holds her M.S.W. from Simmons College.

ADEL AHMED HELMY, of Cairo, Egypt, is an assistant lecturer in Ear, Nose and Throat on the Faculty of Medicine at Benha University, Cairo. She has her M.B., Ch.B., and Master's degrees in Otorhinolaryngology from Al Azhar University, Cairo.

ANNA HOWE, of Parkville, Australia, is a research fellow at the National Research Institute for Gerontology and Geriatric Medicine, Parkville, Victoria. She holds her B.A. and M.A. from Sydney University and her Ph.D. from Monash University and currently is working on a study of the social and economic aspects of retirement.

DAN JACOBSON lives in Tel Aviv, Israel, and is a senior lecturer and Chairperson of the Department of Labour Studies, Tel Aviv University. He holds a Ph.D. in Industrial Relations from the London School of Economics, a B.A. in Sociology and Political Science from the University of Jerusalem, and an M.Sc. from the Israel Institute of Technology, Haifa. He has been a visiting associate professor at Cornell University (1977–1978).

URI LAOR, a resident of Jerusalem, Israel, is Director of the Association for Planning and Development of Services for the Aged (Eshel), Jerusalem, and formerly was Deputy Director of Budget for Social Services, Ministry of Finance (1974–1981). He holds a B.A. in Economics and Sociology and an M.A. in Business Administration from Hebrew University, Jerusalem.

MYRNA I. LEWIS, of New York City, is a psychotherapist and faculty member at Mount Sinai School of Medicine, Department of Community Medicine, New York. She is currently developing a program about older women and health. She holds master's degrees from the University of Minnesota and Columbia University.

JOHN McCALLUM, on sabbatical in Los Angeles, California, is a tenured lecturer at the School of Social and Industrial Administration at Griffith University, Nathan, Australia. At present he is a fellow at the Andrew Norman Institute for Advanced Studies at the University of California. He holds a Ph.D. from Oxford University and has done graduate studies in Economics and Psychology at the University of Queensland, Australia.

SHAFIKA NASSER, a resident of Cairo, Egypt, is a member of the Egyptian Senate, a Professor of Public Health and Nutrition at Cairo University, and an advisor to the National Committee of UNESCO for Environmental Protection. She holds a Ph.D. in Applied Nutrition from the London School of Hygiene and Tropical Medicine, and M.B. and Ch.B. degrees from Cairo University.

LILA NEMESH, of Ramat-Gan, Israel, is a senior physician in the Geriatric Department at Soroka Hospital, Beer Sheva. She has an M.D. from Sackler School of Medicine, Tel-Aviv; has done graduate studies at the University of Vienna, where she holds a certificate in Internal Medicine (1980); and is a tutor in Internal Medicine at Tel-Aviv University.

JANICE NEY, from San Diego, California, is a doctoral student at the University of Southern California, Los Angeles; a member of the American Public Health Association; and former Director of the East County FOCUS Emergency Social Services Project. She holds her B.A. and Master's of Social Work from the University of California and is a graduate student at San Diego State University and Grossmont College.

MAURICIO NORYMBERG, an Argentinian living in Netanya, Israel, is a senior physician of internal medicine at Soroka Medical Center, Beer Sheva. He earned his M.D. at the University of Buenos Aires. He has specialized in cardiology and internal medicine in Buenos Aires and Israel (1977–1979).

HELENA PONTES CARREIRA is a resident of Lisbon, Portugal, and is a technical officer with the Department of Studies and Health Planning, Lisbon. She is a graduate of the Technical School for Infirmaries and the Institute for Applied Psychology, Lisbon; and is doing postgraduate studies at the Universities of Leeds and Bangor, U.K.

CATHERINE PSAROULI, of Athens, Greece, is Deputy Director of the National Welfare Organization, Day Care Community Center, Peristeri, Greece. She is a graduate of the School of Social Work, Athens, and worked as a social worker with the Archdiocese of Athens from 1971 to 1975. She participated in the Council of International Programs' seminar in the United States in 1974.

PAULINE ROBINSON lives in Los Angeles, California, and is a research professor of Gerontology at Andrus Gerontology Center, University of Southern California. She holds a Ph.D. in Sociology from the University of California, has done graduate studies at Boston University, and currently is doing research on age, work, and health at the Andrew Norman Advanced Study Institute.

GRAHAM ROWLES, who lives in Morgantown, West Virginia, is an associate professor of Geography at West Virginia University. He holds his Ph.D. from Clark University in Worcester, Massachusetts and has B.A. and M.Sc. degrees from the University of Bristol, England. He has researched and written on the subject, "Environmental Perspectives on Growing Old."

ALIPIO SANCHEZ-VIDAL, of Barcelona, Spain, is a psychologist and doctoral student at the University of Barcelona, from which he received a degree in Engineering. He holds an M.A. in Psychology from the University of Minnesota and has done graduate studies at the University of Michigan and clinical work at university hospitals in Minnesota and South Carolina, Stillwater State Prison, Minneapolis Health Center, and other U.S. institutions.

EDUARDO SERRA, a resident of Lisbon, Portugal, is Adjoint Secretary of State for Employment at the Ministry of Labour, Lisbon; and is a consulting psychologist at the General Office of Medical Aid, Ministry of Education and Culture. He graduated with a degree in Social Psychology from Sorbonne University, Paris, and Superior Institute of Psychology, Lisbon.

ADA SHER, of Chapel Hill, North Carolina, is a doctoral student at the University of North Carolina, Chapel Hill; a former research assistant at Harvard School of Dental Medicine and Georgia Institute of Technology; and currently is coordinating a seminar on international health and preparing a case-study trip to China.

MARIA SJENITZER-BIERSTEE lives in Utrecht, Holland, and is a lecturer at the Institute for Educational Psychology and Utrecht General Hospital. She holds a Doctorate in Clinical Psychology and is a member of the Dutch Institute of Psychologists and the Association for Behavioral Therapy.

DAVID VANCE, a resident of Bangor, Northern Ireland, is Principal Social Worker (training and staff development) at Eastern Health and Social Services Board, Bangor. He holds an M.A. in Social Sciences from Brunel University, Uxbridge and a Bachelor of Social Sciences from Queen's University, Belfast. He teaches social work at Ulster Polytechnic and the New University.

MARK WILLIAMS, of Rochester, New York, is an assistant professor of Medicine (Geriatrics) at the University of Rochester and a staff member and the Medical Director of the Geriatric Consultative Service, Monroe Community Hospital. He holds A.B. and M.D. degrees from the University of North Carolina.

WLODARCZYK WLODZIMIERZ lives in Lodz, Poland, and heads the Organization and Management Section at the Institute of Occupational Medicine, Lodz. He graduated in Law, Organization, and Management from the University of Warsaw, has been an advisor to the World Health Organization, and currently is involved in reorganizing the social health system in Poland.

Health, Productivity, and Aging: An Overview

Robert N. Butler

This is the century of old age or, as it has been called, the Age of Aging. It is the first century in which a human being can be expected (at least in those countries where the potential has been realized) more often than otherwise to live out what we presently think of as the life course. It is the first period in history when any child can expect to attain old age. There is an unprecedented increase in the absolute number and relative proportion of older persons. The age structure of society is changing, and this is true not just in the First and Second Worlds, but in the Third World as well. Population aging is a worldwide phenomenon. By the year 2000 there will be a doubling of the present number of persons in the world over 60. And 60 percent of those over 60 will reside in the developing world. Old age, historically the privilege of the few, has become the destiny of the many.

To attain some sense of the triumph of survival, consider the history of the United States. The United States once was a Third World nation. In 1830 only one-third of newborn infants survived into their sixties; today, over 80 percent do. In 1870, just 115 years ago, only 44 percent of women who survived past the age of 15, who did not die of diphtheria or chicken pox, lived out what we presently would think of as the natural, normal life course. In 1920 a 10 year old in the United States had only a 40-percent chance of having two of four grandparents alive; today that child has a 75-percent chance. In 1900, the average life expectancy was 47; today it is 73, a gain of 26 years. This nearly equals the 29 years gained in average life expectancy from the Bronze Age—3000 B.C.—to 1900 A.D. In the United States and in many other parts of the world, the fastest-growing age group is 85 and over.

This is also the century for older women. Women have made progress in suffrage, in education, and employment. They often have been in the vanguard of human change. Nonetheless, at present, women are the world's poorest of the poor.

Remarkable as the increase in average life expectancy in the United States has been in this century, we certainly must remind ourselves that the developing world's peoples do not experience and enjoy the same life expectancy. Within all countries, developing and developed, there also are those who, because of socioeconomic status, race, or ethnicity, do not enjoy the same life expectancy.

This is not only the century of old age, but the century of the multigenerational family. I think how often during my years of clinical practice I have seen a 90 year old who might be taking care of a 70 year old. In the United States, for example, of the 80 percent of all persons over 65 who have a living child, 94 percent are grandparents and 46 percent are great-grandparents.

I have said that one should applaud and celebrate these changes, yet we see and hear much concern: First, there is the concern for dependency—specifically, economic dependency—and the high costs of health care and income maintenance. There is a special sub-class of fears of dependency, related to particular forms of debility. One might call it the Struldbrug Effect. The Struldbrugs, whom Gulliver discovered on one of his travels, live forever, but unfortunately also become increasingly decrepit. Especially frightening is senility. Until the various forms of senility, and most particularly senile dementia of the Alzheimer type, have been conquered, the specter of senility is likely to continue to dominate and shape perceptions, attitudes, and fears with regard to old age.

Second, there is a failure to understand the underlying mechanisms of aging, to recognize the distinctions between natural life span and life expectancy. Life span, the genetically determined inherent life span of a species, is not clearly distinguished from the survivorship of the species. Most of us tend to forget yesterday's conquests. In the United States, a polio epidemic was last experienced 22 years ago, yet very few of us are conscious of this reality. Indeed, it is often necessary to remind people to promote proper vaccination.

Third, and perhaps most important, is a psychological problem that I regard as nearly universal—the difficulty in maintaining a connection between our present self and our future self. Marcel Proust wrote, "Old age perhaps of all the realities is the one we preserve longest in our life as a truly abstract conception." We continue to associate morbidity and mortality with age; therefore, we assume that the increase in life expectancy will increase disproportionately the costs of health care and income maintenance. The last illness has always been the most expensive. It is not that longevity has extended the period of incapacity; rather, it is our inability to adjust our expectations and environments so as to encourage and allow elderly people to exercise their capacities.

Unless we can begin to perceive older persons as productive, their lives will be at risk. They will be seen as a burden. How will the threshold of burden be defined? Will *triage*, the French term derived from battlefield conditions in World War I, be transposed to peacetime conditions to select for elimination certain less "effective" or productive groups within a society—older people, the disabled, and the like? In some respects I would contend that in the United States covert euthanasia already is operating in emergency rooms and in many situations in which it is not always conscious. Physicians and health providers are often making decisions with regard to dying and death without the participation of older persons or their families. We have long seen in the United States hostile terms applied to older citizens and middle-aged women by physicians, terms that may not be familiar internationally: "gomer," which is an acronym for "Get out of my emergency room," or "gork," "God only really knows." Nor are "dirtball," "vegetable," or "crock" terms of endearment. Those elements of an extraordinarily insensitive medical lexicon clearly express the helplessness physicians and other providers feel in the face of untreatable malady, particularly those who adopt divine pretensions.

There is, of course, much of value in the concept of the right to die with dignity; however, there are dangers that we are beginning to see. In the United Kingdom, the Society for the Right to Die is actively encouraging suicide. France, too, has actively debated the propriety of the suicide manual entitled *Self Deliverance*, published in 1982 by Michel Linda. In California, Hemlock, an organization of some growing popularity, is actively encouraging suicide by the terminally ill. In 1977 *The Washington Post* revealed an "in-house" pol-

icy paper within the Department of Health, Education, and Welfare
that suggested(the need to encourage older persons in the United
States to sign "right to die" cards in order to reduce "heroic measures" undertaken in the terminal care of older persons and thereby
curb costs.) It comes close to the concept of the "final solution."
Professor Anthony DeBono, a leading figure in the 1982 U.N. World
Assembly on Aging, has expressed directly his own personal fear that
active euthanasia soon will be applied, as the crunch of numbers of
older persons approaches.

There are no data, in the United States at least, to support the
widely held notion, or misperception, that there are growing conflicts
between young and old. The data of the Louis Harris polling organization does not show a war between the generations, a phrase used
in the American Media, including the big news magazines. The
French demographer Alfred Sauvy (1984) sees the aging of society as
much more serious than the North/South struggle. He has related the
rise of the number of older persons to the decline of Periclean
Greece. His view of the graying of France and, by extension, the
graying of nations, approaches the apocalyptic. There are those who
see a "gray peril."

In May 1982, I attended a Commonwealth Fund Forum in London on "Improving the Health of the Homebound Elderly: The Best
Prospects for Five English-speaking Countries." Representatives of
the United Kingdom, Canada, the United States, New Zealand, and
Australia were asked the question: "Is there a collision course between projected public expenditures for the elderly and other national priorities?"

Karen Davis, a U.S. health economist and official in the Carter
Administration, has predicted a collision course in the United States
unless there are effective interventions. She pointed to the U.S. federal budget, 21 percent of which is devoted to defense and 9 percent
to debt service, for a total of 30 percent. By 1985 the defense budget
will have moved up to 28 percent and debt service to 13 percent, for
a total of 41 percent. In other words, in two years those two elements
alone will gobble up 11 percent more of the national budget. Social
Security needs, especially Medicare benefits, are expected to increase during the same period.

Joseph Califano, both during and following his tenure as Secretary of Health, Education, and Welfare, was particularly vehement in raising the specter of the "graying of the budget" in the United States. He warned constantly that Social Security would go bankrupt and that health costs associated with aging were simply unsupportable. Califano and other politicians expressed despair over the alleged freezing of the share of national wealth by entitlement programs—uncontrollable, nondiscretionary, or committed portions of national budgets. Of course, politicians despair about this in part because entitlement programs freeze their own capacity to make decisions and to act.

National magazines such as *Forbes* and *Newsweek* frequently have carried jeremiads regarding the costs and burdens of an aging population. A typical example was the January 24, 1983 issue of *Newsweek* that quite inaccurately showed on its cover one young person holding up nine people older than himself. The title was, "The Social Security Crisis, Who Will Pay? The Growing Burden on the Young." It also clearly indicates the failure to perceive the connection between our future selves and our present selves, that the social security burden upon the young is a reflection of the ultimate opportunity for the young person when he gets old to receive appropriate and necessary support.

A 1983 article in *The New York Times,* reporting on a meeting of the American Association for the Advancement of Science, noted that "life expectancy in the United States is increasing so dramatically today that taxpayers in the coming years may have to come up with billions of additional dollars to support the aged". The article attributes this problem largely to "a drop in deaths from heart disease and stroke in the last decade in the United States." I wonder if anyone would suggest that we cease and desist from continuing biomedical research in the National Heart, Blood and Lung Institute.

Barbara Boyle Torrey and Douglas Norwood, economists with the Federal Office of Management and Budget, in a 1983 article in *The New York Times* also have warned that improvements in mortality rates would increase the already ominous growth potential in costs of programs for the aged. They have urged consideration of such options as extending the retirement age or reimbursing the government from the estates of those who die after long lives.

Many of these concerns, of course, are operative not only in the United States. They arise in Europe and elsewhere. We know, too, from field reports, that, with urbanization in Africa, Latin America, and Asia, older people, particularly women, frequently have been left in the villages, often in poverty. There has been a tendency for many of the representatives of the nations of Latin America, Asia, and Africa to deny that there is a serious problem, perhaps because they haven't reached the "burden" threshold in percentage of older persons. They take understandable pride in the value of the extended family system. But some voices, for example Nana Apt's of Ghana at the United Nations World Assembly on Aging in Vienna, July 1982, very forthrightly warn of present and future dangers.

As both T. S. Eliot and George Orwell have reminded us, the past and future really exist in the present. In this century we have seen totalitarian movements; titanic struggles between East and West, North and South; massive disputes over what type of socioeconomic and political system in which to live; unprecedented advances in scientific technology and global communication; new developments in what we may call the "new biology," including techniques of recombinant DNA or cloning, hybridoma technology, and a flourishing body of neuroscience. We see major unemployment around the world, 10 percent in the United States, over 11 percent in European nations. R. J. Barnet wrote in *The Lean Years* (1980), "What do we do about the surplus population, to use a phrase from Dickens' time, is the number one problem for political leaders around the world, and, in a condition of scarcity, managing societies made up of millions of people without jobs, money or hope, invites draconian economics and brutal policies." He goes on:

> Fewer and fewer have a chance to be regarded as productive, the reserve army of the unemployable is becoming so vast—perhaps as many as a billion [worldwide], that it not only keeps wages depressed but also begins to create social instability. . . . [We live in] the age of scarcity, [where] the expendability of human life and the waste of human potential [are] direct consequences of the sort of economic development being pursued in most parts of the world. An increasing proportion of the world's population is becoming irrelevant to the productive process. Automation has dramatically reduced the number of hands needed to make what the world wants, and because of the new mobility of the post World War II multinational corporation, many of the jobs that remain are concentrated in low-wage enclaves in a few poor countries. . . . In the United States, the consequences of the "life boat ethic" are already visible; the vast wasteland of decay in every major city in which the poor

are concentrated; the depressed rural areas, no longer needed to produce the nation's food. We are reaching the point where some of our
most basic beliefs about human life will have to be tested. We will be
forced either to bring our economic institutions into line with the fundamental humanistic and democratic values we profess or openly reject
them in favor of the life boat ethic."

We can see how far we are from facing that question by looking
at the competition for resources brought on by an extraordinarily
rekindled nuclear arms race. Such militarization absorbs incredible
resources. Isn't it ironic that, at the very moment when survivorship
is increasing, we face the growing possibility of thermonuclear ex-
tinction?

I believe there is an alternative. Before advancing it, however, I
must discuss the words we are using. *Aging, health,* and *productivity*
all relate to socioeconomic status, particularly to occupation and education, to national origin and residence, and to race and ethnicity.

Aging is a process, to be distinguished from a stage or a group,
defined, say, in terms of entitlements. From the biological or biomedical perspective, aging is a predictable, progressive, universal
deterioration in various physiological systems, mental and physical,
behavioral and biomedical. At the same time there is clear evidence,
though more elusive and more difficult to measure, of concurrent
psychosocial growth in capacities for strategy, sagacity, prudence,
wisdom, seasoning, and experience. We must distinguish between
population aging and individual aging. The age structure of a society
is a function of birth rates, death rates, and migration. Birth and
death rates in turn are a function of socioeconomic conditions, including the stage of medical progress and its application in public health
measures. In a sense, population aging begins in the bedroom and is
reinforced by the laboratory and the clinic.

Health, I suggest, as does the World Health Organization, must
be seen in terms of being "a state of complete physical, mental, and
social well-being, not merely the absence of disease or infirmity"
(*Public Health Report,* 1946). Much discussion of health, at least in
the United States, is really a discussion of medicine. The medical
model is a very constricted one. Only relatively recently has attention
been drawn to the elements of health promotion and disease prevention, a movement toward a broader social definition of health.

Productivity, as an economic term, refers to individual or collective creation of a product or service over a unit of time. It is necessary to find primarily the kinds of productivity that societies perceive and benefit from. For example, is the so-called Gross National Product necessarily a function of individual or collective benefit? The Gross National Product includes pollution and other disadvantageous elements in its measurement. The relationship between those who control the systems of productivity and the ultimate social good is critical. Whether productivity is dominated by individual, entrepreneurial, or state capitalism, there has yet to be a successful diffusion or dissemination of benefits to a really broad membership of particular societies. Productivity does not simply mean making objects. There must be an increase in the basic wealth of the country. Jobs, then, must mean wealth. In the United States, jobs must include some awareness of the shift over to a service-dominated economy, because today more U.S. jobs are related to the service sector than to the manufacturing sector. A major task is to reevaluate the very meaning of productivity. We cannot be satisfied with prevailing conceptions.

As an alternative to the "lifeboat" dilemma, where the ship is perceived to be sinking and only a select few are given the chance to survive, I believe that significant numbers of people over 60 and 65 can in fact continue to work and contribute to their communities. There are data from a few longitudinal studies in the United States— the National Institutes of Health, the National Institute on Aging, and Duke University—demonstrating that cognitive abilities in older persons, speaking very broadly, decline less and later than originally had been reported in earlier studies. The presence of decrements requires a diagnostic evaluation for possible pathological explanation. There are also data regarding educability and dependability of older workers. Despite stereotypes in the United States, at any one moment only 5 percent of those 65 or over are in any kind of an institution. There are comparable figures from European and other Western nations. Of all those who survive past 65 in the United States, only about 20 to 25 percent will have any kind of an institutional experience, however brief. Let's put it a little more positively. At any one moment, 95 percent of older persons reside in the community and 80 percent of those who survive past 65 will never have any kind of an institutional experience. There are myriad personal examples of extraordinarily able and contributing older persons.

What is the relationship between an increase in average life expectancy and work ability? During my tenure as director of the National Institute on Aging, I was asked by the United States Commission on Social Security Reform to address that question. It's not a simple question. In the United States the data from the National Center of Health Statistics, for example, indicate an increased disability, or morbidity, with each decade of life. There is certainly a large subpopulation of increasingly healthy, educated, activist, vigorous older persons who can enhance their own and society's well-being through productivity.

In my book, *Why Survive? Being Old in America* (Butler, 1975), I developed an "Agenda for Activism" that has been used by the Gray Panthers and other organizations on a local level. It includes such basic activities as:

1. Consciousness and conscience raising
2. Politics: organizing, becoming delegates to political party conventions, conducting registration drives to be certain that older people can vote
3. Community activity; such as membership by older persons on boards of trustees of nursing homes
4. Legal activity: starting class-action suits and using Social Security grievance procedures
5. Collective activity: organizing to meet and represent the needs of the elderly
6. Protective activity: arranging escort services for the elderly in high-crime areas
7. Surveillance of nursing homes and other facilities
8. Cooperative activity: forming food, drug, insurance, travel, and other purchasing cooperatives
9. Communication and education: obtaining regular TV, radio, and newspaper time.

There is need, too, for a politics of aging. To be politically effective, such a movement must attain certain thresholds:

1. A certain number and proportion of older persons
2. A certain percentage of disability-free older persons with an adequate level of energy
3. Enough older leaders and models

4. Reduced denial of age by healthy and affluent older persons who otherwise do not identify with the sick and poor
5. Improvement in the role of the media and education in combating the unfortunate stereotypes and devalued images of age
6. Mobilization of anger and outrage against the tacit repression of old people comparable to that aroused by women and racial minorities
7. Disciplined support for political candidates who are genuinely committed to changing attitudes and policies toward the elderly.

There must be a close alliance with the women's movement, especially emphasizing the powerful twin facts of the feminization of aging and the feminization of poverty. Until recently, the women's movement has had other concerns and has not given much attention to issues affecting its older sisters.

Finally, there must be intergenerational alliances. The baby boomers, born between 1946 and 1964, comprise the largest generation in U.S. history. They are now between 20 and 38 years of age and number some 70 million. They are not especially concerned with the problems of aging and are not devoting much attention to studying them. From the poll results, including the Harris Poll, young people do favor Social Security and expanded benefits of all types for older persons. Yet many of them do not believe that they will receive those benefits when they grow old. We must strengthen their awareness of connections between their present and future selves.

To mobilize the skills and talents of older persons will benefit both older persons and society. At present, no government or private institution within society has addressed effectively and comprehensively the multiple challenges posed by societal aging. There has been progress, of course, of varying degrees in different countries, including the development of social security programs, social services, research, and education. These efforts, both in the United States and elsewhere, may be at some risk in part because of austerity or alleged austerity. Certainly none of them are perfect.

Population aging is significant, though not quite so powerful as might be thought. We should note the actual distribution by age group, decade by decade. The median age of societies is not rising so dramatically as one might think. I have been guilty of using phrases like the "graying of America." I think we are overdoing it. There is a tendency for any of us who are trying to highlight an issue in the United States to be overly dramatic. The efforts of the supporters of cancer research may have contributed to a certain degree of cancer-phobia. And right now those of us who were anxious to sharpen attention upon Alzheimer's disease are becoming aware of the extent to which overdiagnoses are being made. Some people are being frightened into thinking that if they can't remember something on their 51st birthday they're in trouble. So we always have to be careful as we highlight significant issues.

As I have stated earlier, the great gains in life expectancy are yet to come. If the inherent life span of humankind hovers around 110, we have a long way to go from an average life expectancy of 73. So population aging or the demographic revolution as seen so far may be somewhat overstated. Important as it is, it's a modest force in the worldwide economic situation. We need to understand the interactions among population aging, health, and productivity, but we must approach them within this larger context.

It seems to me there are certain nonsolutions. We certainly don't want to return to the era of high mortality or high birth rates. We certainly don't want to blame the victim. We *do* want to enhance the productive potential of older persons and reduce their dependency. I suggest the following agenda:

1. Enhance cultural and moral sensitivity to older people or, more precisely, to the human life cycle.
2. Smash stereotypes and rectify the many distortions that dominate and plague so-called policy debates; this may be done through public education and studies of healthy older persons.
3. Reconceptualize or humanize our concepts of productivity.
4. Enhance societal productivity through investments in science and technology, particularly in health and education.
5. Enhance individual productivity through national planning, through wrestling in a meaningful way with the setting of priorities.
6. Increase disability-free life expectancy, a different type of life expectancy, through health promotion and disease prevention.

7. Alter work conditions and work tasks and look for new work forms.
8. Break down the now ironclad compartments of education for the young, work for the middle aged, and retirement for the old.
9. Examine the notion of separating income from work itself and support activities that are equivalent in socioeconomic value to agreed-upon examples of productivity.
10. Value and use wisdom.
11. Look at the role of the family in strengthening productivity.
12. Share our technological success with everyone.
13. Convert management thinking about retirees and older workers: People should not be thrown away; they have important contributions to make.
14. Recognize that health and productivity are interacting conditions: The unproductive human is at higher risk of illness and economic dependency and the sick person is limited in productivity and is, therefore, at higher risk of dependency.

REFERENCES AND BIBLIOGRAPHY

Barnet, R. J. (1980). *The lean years: Politics in the age of scarcity*. New York: Simon and Schuster.

Birren, E., Butler, R. N., Greenhouse, S. W., Sokoloff, L., & Yarrow, M. R. (1963). *Human aging: A biological and behavioral study*. U.S. Public Health Service, Publication No. 986. Washington, D.C.: U.S. Government Printing Office. Reprinted 1971, 1974.

Butler, R.N. (1963). The life review: An interpretation of reminiscence in the aged. *Psychiatry, 26*, 65–76.

Butler, R. N. (1969). Ageism: Another form of bigotry. *The Gerontologist, 9*, 243–246.

Butler, R. N. (1970). Old age dividends for lifetime investments in America. *Aging and Human Development, 1*, 1975–1985.

Butler, R. N. (1975). *Why Survive? Being Old in America*. New York: Harper & Row.

Club of Rome/Meadows, D.H., Meadows, D. L., Randers, J., Jr., & Behrens, W. W., III. (1972). *The limits of growth*. Washington, D.C.: Potomac Associates.

DeGrazia, S. (1964). *Of time, work and leisure*. Garden City, N.Y.: Anchor Books.

Gleason, H. (Ed.) (1980). *Getting better, A report on health care from the Salzburg Seminar*. Cambridge, Mass.: Oelgeschlager, Gunn & Hain.

National Institute on Aging. (1982). *A national plan for research on aging toward an independent old age*. NIH Publication 82–2453. Washington, D.C.: National Institutes of Health.

Sauvy, A. (1984). Effets intellectuels et moraux du viellissement d'une population. In J. Wertheismer and M. Morris (Eds.), *Senile dementia: Outlook for the future*. New York: Alan R. Liss.

Simon, J. (1984). *The ultimate resource*. Princeton, N.J.: Princeton University Press.

World Health Organization. (1946). Constitution of the World Health Organization. *Public Health Report, 61*:1268–1277.

Yoshitomi, M. (1982, July 14). A weak spot for Japanese. *The New York Times*, p. D2.

2

Biomedical and Environmental Influences on Aging

Alvar Svanborg

In medicine, there has been, and still is, a tendency to comprehend aging of old people as something pathological. Yet we all consider growth and functional improvement in the first phase of the lifespan to be normal processes. Why shouldn't we consider other phases of the lifespan, such as morphological and functional decline in aging, as normal? It also may be that dying is caused by normal aging processes, although most death certificates, at least in developed countries, describe one or more sophisticated medical diagnoses as the cause of death.

It is well known that the risk of falling ill increases in old age. In clinical medicine we are used to statements implying that if a doctor examines people at the age of 70 and above carefully enough he will find that "they are all ill in one way or another." Old *and* sick! Is this the reality? No; as Gershwin wrote, "It ain't necessarily so!"

In everyday clinical work we define the terms *healthy, well*, or *less well* according to clinically observable disorders. We know, however, that a really clear delineation between health and disease is not possible. The older the patient the more difficult such a delineation will become, because aging may cause impairments, disabilities, and handicaps similar to those caused by disease. The border zone becomes broader at higher ages. The identification of manifestations of aging and of symptoms of many definable disorders in the elderly requires not only knowledge of possible change in the symptomatology and natural course of disease at old age but also observations during longer periods of time.

15

The problem of distinguishing between physiological aging and definable disorders has in recent time become even more difficult but also more challenging. We seem just now to live in a period of human history when both the rate and/or manifestations of aging and state of health are undergoing marked and rapid changes. The vitality of old people in Sweden today seems to be greater than what it was only five to 10 years ago. In other words, we are experiencing rapidly occurring age cohort differences. These age cohort differences are obvious effects of a changing environment. Indirectly we now also can begin to define possible active preventive/postponing measures aimed at improving even further our vitality and health as we grow old.

I want to describe some of our research findings concerning

1. The nature and manifestations of aging. We have studied people at age 70 and above in Gothenburg, Sweden (for reviews, see Rinder, Roupe, Steen, & Svanborg, 1975; Svanborg, 1977; Svanborg, Bergström, & Mellström, 1982; Svanborg, Landahl, & Mellström, 1982). Two other studies at younger ages in the same population (Bengtsson et al., 1973; Tibblin, 1967), in which some of the methodology has been identical, have also allowed certain retrospective longitudinal considerations and conclusions.
2. The occurrence and nature of impairment, disability, and handicap due to aging itself, but also the incidence and prevalence of definable disorders in the elderly. To what extent are the elderly still vital and healthy enough to be able to contribute in a productive way, or to what extent are they mainly care consumers?
3. The possibilities for preventive/postponing activities. Obviously, measuring them is of great importance in this context.

The entire combined population of the Nordic countries was in 1982 the longest lived in the world, although male Japanese now live longest and Japanese females did so in 1983. In Sweden, the percentage of those aged 65 and over is at the present time approaching 17 percent of a population of about 8.13 million. The predictions for the next 40 years indicate with certain variations from time to time a further increase, of those 65 and over, both absolutely and relatively, of at least 20 percent in the year 2025. As in many other populations, the increase of the oldest olds will be the most pronounced. During the period 1970 to the year 2000, the absolute number of those 85 and over will have doubled, while those 95 and over will have tripled, implying a dramatic increase in the need for social support and medical service to the elderly in Sweden. Such a shift in the composition of our population also means that in the future one-fifth of the population will put great demands both on care programs and on societal planning in general. We will have to adjust better both to the need for support of the elderly and to their demand for continued meaningful, productive, and responsible contribution to society.

What follows is based to a great extent upon results obtained in our gerontological and geriatric longitudinal study of 70 year olds in Gothenburg, Sweden.

Gothenburg is situated on the West Coast of Sweden. It is the second largest city in the country, with 450,000 inhabitants in the downtown area and approximately one million people in the metropolitan area. It is rather heavily industrialized and has the biggest harbor in the country and a well-developed school and university life. The objectives, design (see Table 2.1), sampling, and performance of the longitudinal study of 70 year olds, which was done in 1971 and 1972, have been described previously (Rinder et al, 1975; Svanborg, 1977). Follow-up studies were performed in 1976 and 1977 at age 75, in 1980 and 1981 at age 79, and in 1982 and 1983 at age 81. In 1976 and 1977, an age cohort comparison was made with another group of 70 year olds, later followed up in 1981 and 1982 at the age of 75. Because of the rather marked cohort differences we observed both at age 70 and 75, a third age cohort of 70 year olds is under investigation at the present time (Table 2.1). It should be emphasized that the systematically sampled groups of 70 year olds have been shown to be representative of the total population of 70 year olds. The results obtained, therefore, can be generalized to the total population.

BIOMEDICAL INFLUENCES

According to our general notion about aging, life has only two phases: (1) growth and functional improvement or (2) somatic wither (atrophy) and functional decline. There are in fact certain functional parameters that show almost a two-phase curve between functional ability and

TABLE 2.1.   Design of the longitudinal population study of 70 year olds in Gothenburg, Sweden.

Date of Birth	Year of Investigation				
	1971/1972	1976/1977	1980/1981	1981/1982	1982/1983
1901/1902	70 years	75 years	79 years		81 years
1906/1907		70 years		75 years	
1912/1913				70 years	

Source: Svanborg, A.: p. 175. In Caird, F.I. & Grimley Evans, J. (Eds.): Advanced geriatric medicine 3. The Pitman Press, Bath, 1983. Used by permission of Pitman Publishing Ltd., London.

chronological age. A typical example is the perceptual speed (the psychomotive speed) that begins to go down between the ages of 20 and 30. Due to reasons not wholly understood, the basal oxygen consumption also starts to decline almost linearly, early in life.

But for many other functions the relationship between functional performance and chronological age shows a curve that generally can be considered to imply at least four phases (see Figure 2.1). After the first phase of growing and functional improvement, there is a period of life of at least the same duration when functional ability seems to be rather constant or declining only slightly. This second phase is then followed by a third phase with functional decline commonly at a rate of 1 percent per year (Svanborg, Landahl, & Mellström, 1982.) Finally, there seems to exist in some individuals also a terminal phase when the appearance and aggravation of manifestations of aging increase and vitality rapidly goes down.

Most organs, presumably all of them, have a marked reserve capacity, with only about 20 percent of the total organ function capacity ordinarily used at younger ages. This reserve capacity declines with increasing age. The rate of decline of different organ functions is, however, impossible or extremely difficult to analyze, especially in humans. It is difficult to state to what extent in the final and terminal aging phase, predicted by our present experiences from the longitudinal study of 70 year olds as well as from clinical experiences, we have reached a phase of life when we have no reserve capacity whatsoever.

The length of the second phase with a rather stationary functional period is different for different functions. The composition of muscle fibers in the striated muscles and their enzyme composition have been reported to be rather unchanged, indicating an unchanged

FIGURE 2.1.   Relationship between Functional Performance and Chronological Age.

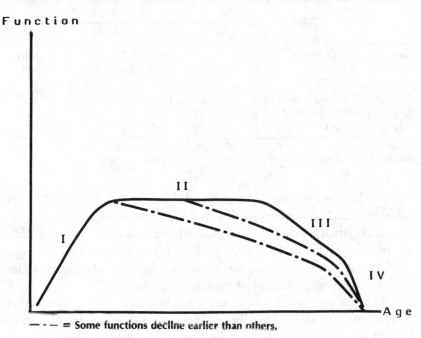

— - — = Some functions decline earlier than others,

qualitative functional ability up to age 60 (Grimby, Danneskoid-Sam-
soe, Hvid, & Saltin, 1982). Studies of the immune response in our
own samples of 70 year olds indicate no measurable decline in immune response until after age 70 (BJursten, Bergström, & Svanborg,
1985), and studies of body compositions show only very small changes
in the Gothenburg population up to age 65 in males and 70 in females
(Steen, Bruce, Isaksson, Lewin, & Svanborg, 1977).

Many of these differences in levels and curves for different organ
functions have important clinical consequences. They also have significant effects in the productive ability of the elderly. For example,
many studies definitely show that, except for the psychomotive
speed, measurable cognitive abilities are well preserved in healthy
elderly up to at least age 70 to 75 (Berg, 1980; Botwinick, 1977;
Schaie & Labouvie-Vief, 1974). The study of 70 year olds (Berg, 1980;
Svanborg, Berg, Nilsson, & Persson, 1984) found a positive cohort
difference implying that the 70 year olds of 1976 and 1977 were even
more intellectually able than those who became 70 years old in 1971

TABLE 2.2.   Intelligence and memory test results among 70-year-old people in Gothenburg, Sweden, 1971/1972 and 1976/1977, cohort comparison.

	1971/72			1976/77				
	$\bar{x}$	S.D.	N.	$\bar{x}$	S.D.	N.	t	p <
Verbal meaning/SRB 1	17.0	6.4	337	18.5	6.7	387	3.18	.001
Reasoning/SRB2	12.6	4.6	359	13.9	4.8	392	6.60	.001
Spatial ability/SRB 3	12.9	6.3	181	15.5	7.3	398	6.96	.001
Perceptual speed/Ps—if	15.4	8.2	184	19.1	7.1	391	5.48	.001
Digits forward	5.6	1.0	178	5.4	1.2	398	1.98	NS
Digits backward	3.8	0.9	178	4.1	1.2	397	2.96	.01

Source: Berg, S. et al: Acta Psychiat. Scand. Suppl. 288, Vol. 62, 1980. © 1980 Munksgaard International Publishers Ltd., Copenhagen, Denmark.

and 1972, only five years earlier (see Table 2.2). It is a paradox in our societies that the intellectual function of the elderly improves but the economic situation and technological advances minimize the availability of meaningful professional activities for them. So, too, in many modern societies, the increase in further life expectancy coincides with a reduction in the age of mandatory retirement.

As far as age cohort differences are concerned, there is both direct and indirect evidence for future changes. Examples are the well-known changes in longevity and in height and body weight in many countries. In Gothenburg our studies revealed dental changes (Österberg, Hedegård, & Säther, 1983) as well as a general trend toward a better state of health in the second 70-year-old cohort compared to the first one examined. We also have found indirect evidence of coming cohort differences. Both smoking (Mellström, Rundgren, Jagenburg, Steen, & Svanborg, 1982) and alcohol abuse (Mellstrom, Rundgren, & Svanborg, 1981) have been found to be negatively related to muscle strength, density of the skeleton, and to the balance of gonadal steroid hormones, indicating that these lifestyle factors increase the rate and manifestation of aging in these respects. Further generations of elderly will include a higher percentage of smokers and people who have smoked for longer periods of their lives than the cohorts we have studied already.

Up to now we have found only one negative trend as far as age cohort differences are concerned—a rapid, ongoing increase of the age-adjusted incidence of hip fractures (Zetterberg & Andersson, 1982). If this trend cannot be changed it will have serious human and economic consequences, implying that twice as many elderly will suffer from hip fractures in the year 2000 than can be explained only by the changes of the age structure of the population. Many observations indicate, however, that positive changes of lifestyle factors such as improved physical activity, adequate intake of calcium, regular exposure to ultraviolet light even at old age, as well as lower consumption of tobacco and alcohol will have a preventive/postponing effect on the age-related decline of the skeleton, and obviously then also on the risk of broken arms and legs. To what extent these observations also will increase the indications for postmenopausal substitution therapy with gonadal steroids is a question of urgent importance.

The more we know about the rate and manifestations of aging at about 70 years, the more we realize how common are misdiagnoses at these ages. Underdiagnosis is common, implying that the elderly are suffering from impairment, disability, or handicap that they themselves don't even mention to the doctor, because they comprehend the symptoms as manifestations of aging (Svanborg, 1977). One example in our study was urinary incontinence, which is very common in females but very seldom mentioned, investigated, or treated. Furthermore, several symptoms become less pronounced at old age, and the symptomatology is, therefore, more vague. Examples are the rise in body temperature with infections and pain, for example, myocardial infarctions and acute abdominal disorders. Contrary to what most people believe, including many members of the medical profession, both correct diagnosis and adequate treatment of older persons often are more difficult and presuppose even more knowledge of and experience in the handling of geriatric patients than in the handling of patients at younger adult ages.

An even greater clinical problem is overdiagnosis of the elderly. Limited knowledge of how aging manifests itself allows interpretation of those manifestations as symptoms of disease. Examples are age-related changes in blood pressure and blood glucose level, misdiagnosed as hypertensive disease and diabetes, respectively. Shortness of breath during exercise and a tendency to water retention in the legs are also common in healthy elderly people but increase the risk for overdiagnosis of congestive heart failure.

Finally, rather common disorders in old age such as acute infections and traumatic injuries can suddenly lower the physical and/or mental capacity of an individual down to a performance level that implies helplessness and advanced handicap. In such situations early and correct diagnosis and treatment are even more urgently needed than at younger ages, when an individual has greater reserves. They depend on wider knowledge of really definable disorders and their possible treatment in old age.

ENVIRONMENTAL INFLUENCES

We are all aware of the fact that our environment and lifestyle influence our state of health. Nowadays we dare to state that these factors also influence the rate and manifestations of aging and the functional consequences of these manifestations. To what extent would it be possible at least to postpone impairment, disability, and handicap?

These questions are obviously extremely complex. I cannot produce firm statements, but I have some ideas based mainly on observations that we have made in our longitudinal studies of representative samples of 70 year olds. The age cohort differences observed in our study, as well as others, must be due mainly to environmental influences, since reasons to believe in the influence of genetic changes are lacking. There is both direct and indirect evidence of cohort differences. The most obvious is the marked changes in longevity as well as the ongoing increase in further life expectancy at ages above 65. During the many decades in Sweden when infant mortality was low and declining only slightly, there was a marked further increase in life expectancy at several adult ages. Since World War II, longevity has increased by no less than seven years in females and 3.5 years in males. A 75-year-old woman alive today can expect to live two years more than a 75-year-old woman could three to four decades ago. Longevity of males at the present time is 72.5 years, six years shorter than in females. It has been rather constant, because prolongation of further life expectancy at ages above 65 has been counterbalanced by an increased death rate in the 45-to-65 age interval.

At the present time, 82 percent of people who die in Sweden are aged 65 or above. Three-quarters of the women who die are aged 72 and above. The corresponding age limit for males is 66 years. In Sweden, it is commonly believed that old people should need only, or at least mainly, general care and social support. We must be aware, however, that the majority of serious and very complicated medical problems nowadays occur in old age. The elderly often need qualified diagnostic resources and therapeutic considerations besides complex medical, psychological, and sociological support. When we consider the possible productivity of the elderly we also should be aware that, at least in Sweden, the average 75-year-old female has almost 11 more years to live and the average male eight more years.

Other examples of age cohort differences are improving intelligence (Table 2.2) and successively improving dental state. A dentist in our research group has reported that 50 percent of the 70 year olds in 1971 and 1972 were lacking their own teeth but that this percentage had decreased to 40 percent in those 70 years old in 1976 and 1977 and to 30 percent in those who were 70 years old in 1981 and 1982.

With regard to other measures of health, our studies have not shown any significant decrease in the prevalence of definable disorders, but altogether the trends indicate an improvement of the state of health in later cohorts.

There is also indirect evidence for future cohort differences. As I pointed out previously, we have observed differences between both smoking and alcohol abuse and muscle strength, skeletal density, and altered gonadal function (Mellström et al., 1981; Mellström et al., 1982). The prevalence of those who for a long period of life have been both smokers and/or alcohol abusers will be higher in coming generations of elderly women, compared to those we have investigated up to now.

We need to find out the reason for the increasing sex difference in rate of aging, state of health, and longevity. In our department we are studying how the obvious sex difference might be explained by ecological factors like smoking and alcohol abuse. The data indicate (Svanborg, Hedenrud, Landahl, Mellström, & Rundgren, 1983) that a considerable part of this sex difference would be explainable by differences in lifestyles, but that the biological prerequisites for a long life are somewhat better in females.

Some disorders, especially gall bladder disease, are related to the number of pregnancies. We already have experienced a declining incidence of gall bladder operations, which might be due at least partly to a lower number of childbirths in the present generation than in previous ones. Future generations of females can then be expected to have even lower incidences of gall bladder disease.

We also know that the living conditions of the elderly have a

TABLE 2.3. Loneliness and subjective health and use of medicines and medical advice in 70 year olds.

	Males			Females			Males + Females		
	Lonely (N = 56) %	Not Lonely (N = 405) %	p	Lonely (N = 129) %	Not Lonely (N = 399) %	p	Lonely (N = 185) %	Not Lonely (N = 804) %	p
Fatigue	37	16	<.001	39	20	<.001	38	18	<.001
Negative self-assessment of health	48	31	<.05	47	32	<.01	47	32	<.001
High consumption of hypnotics and sedatives	20	19	NS	37	23	<.01	32	21	<.01
High frequency of seeking medical advice	29	18	NS	37	25	<.02	34	21	<.001

Source: Berg, S. et al: J. Gerontol. 36:342, 1981. Reprinted by permission of the Journal of Gerontology.

marked influence on vitality and subjective health (Berg, Mellström, Persson, & Svanborg, 1981). Those 70 year olds who were living in a situation where they experienced loneliness as a problem felt more tired, had a worse subjective state of health, and consumed more medical services and drugs than the others (see Table 2.3), although the prevalence of definable somatic disorders was the same as in those without a feeling of loneliness. In the future, with increasing difference in longevity between males and females, even more females may suffer from lack of social contacts to such an extent that a low physical, intellectual, and emotional activity will lower vitality and subjective state of health. One reason for a higher prevalence of affective mental disorders in elderly females than in elderly males is greater frequency of widowhood than widowerhood (Persson, 1980).

In Sweden, bereavement also is associated with a shortening of further life expectancy (Mellström et al., 1982), partly due to the fact that couples often share lifestyles. Recent studies, however, show a dramatic increase in death rate during the first three months after the loss of a spouse; such a sudden increase in morbidity and mortality obviously has other causes than common lifestyle. The mortality rate was found to be no less than 48 percent higher in males and 22 percent higher in females in the age interval 50 to 90 during the first 3 months of bereavement, compared to those still living together with their spouses (Mellström et al., 1982). The marked increase in morbidity and mortality of bereaved spouses during the first year of loneliness warrants intensive study and demands preventive and supportive measures.

New knowledge of aging and the aged seems to show that use of one's physical, mental, and emotional resources improves vitality and functional ability rather than the opposite.

In Chapter 7, I will discuss how we can devote more attention and resources to preventive measures.

REFERENCES AND BIBLIOGRAPHY

Bengtsson, C., Blohmé, G., Hallberg, L., Hällström, T., Isaksson, B., Korsan-Bengtsen, K., Rybo, G., Tibblin, E., Tibblin, G., & Westerberg, H. (1973). The study of women in Gothenburg 1968–1969—A population study. *Acta Med. Scand.*, *193*,311.

Berg, S. (1980). Psychological functioning in 70- and 75-year-old people. A study in an industrialized city. *Acta Psychiat. Scand.* (Suppl. 288), 62.

Berg, S., Mellström, D., Persson, G., & Svanborg, A. (1981). Loneliness in the Swedish aged. *J. Gerontol., 36*,342.

Bjursten, L. M., Bergström, G., & Svanborg, A. (1985). *The immune system in aged humans as judged by in vitro tests in 70- and 75-year-old people*. Unpublished manuscript.

Botwinick, J. (1977). In J. E. Birren & K. W. Schaie (Eds.), *Handbook of the psychology of aging*. New York: Van Nostrand Reinhold.

Grimby, G., Danneskiold-Samsoe, B., Hvid, K., & Saltin, B. (1982). Morphology and enzymatic capacity in arm and leg muscles in 78–82-year-old men and women. *Acta Physiol. Scand., 115*,124.

Mellström, D., Nilsson, A., Oden, A., Rundgren, A., & Svanborg, A. (1982). Mortality among the widowed in Sweden. *Scan. J. Soc. Med., 10*,33.

Mellström, D., Rundgren, A., & Svanborg, A. (1981). Previous alcohol consumption and its consequences for ageing, morbidity and mortality in men aged 70–75. *Age and Ageing, 10*,277.

Mellström, D., Rundgren, A., Jagenburg, R., Steen, B., & Svanborg, A. (1982). Tobacco smoking, ageing and health among the elderly. A longitudinal population study of 70-year-olds and an age cohort comparison. *Age and Ageing, 11*,45.

Österberg, T., Hedegård, B., & Säther, G. (1983). Variation in dental health in 70-year-old men and women in Gothenburg, Sweden. A cross-sectional epidemiological study including longitudinal and cohort effects. *Swed. Dent.J., 7*,29.

Persson, G. (1980). Prevalence of mental disorders in a 70-year-old urban population. *Acta Psychiat. Scand., 62*, 119.

Rinder, L., Roupe, S., Steen, B., & Svanborg, A. (1975). Seventy-year-old people in Gothenburg. A population study in an industrialized Swedish city. I. General presentation of the study. *Acta Med. Scand., 198*, 397.

Schaie, K. W., & Labouvie-Vief, G. V. (1974). *Developmental Psychology, 10*, 305.

Steen, B., Bruce, A., Isaksson, B., Lewin, T., & Svanborg, A. (1977). Body composition in 70-year-old males and females in Gothenburg, Sweden. A population study. *Acta Med. Scand.* (Suppl. 611), 87.

Svanborg, A. (1977). Seventy-year-old people in Gothenburg. A population study in an industrialized Swedish city. II. General presentation of social and medical conditions. *Acta Med. Scand.* (Suppl. 611), 5.

Svanborg, A. (1983). The physiology of ageing in man—Diagnostic and therapeutic aspects. In F. I. Caird & J. Grimley Evans (Eds.), *Advanced geriatric medicine: Vol. 3.* (pp. 175). Bath, England: The Pitman Press.

Svanborg, A., Berg, S., Nilsson, L., & Persson, G. (1984). A cohort comparison of functional ability and mental disorders in two representative samples of 70-year-olds, p. 405. In J. Wertheimer & M. Marois (Eds.), *Modern aging research: Vol 5. Senile dementia: Outlook for the future*. New York: Alan R. Liss Inc.

Svanborg, A., Bergström, G., & Mellström, D. (1982). *Epidemiological studies on social and medical conditions of the elderly. Report on a survey* (EURO reports and studies 62). Copenhagen, Denmark: World Health Organization.

Svanborg, A., Hedenrud, B., Landahl, S., Mellström, D., & Rundgren, A. (1983, March). Skillnaden i forvantad livslangd i olika alderskohorter och mellan man och kvinnor, En belysning av mojliga kausala faktorer. *The Icelandic Medical Journal* (Fylgirit/Supplement 16), 28.

Svanborg, A., Landahl, S., & Mellström, D. (1982). Basic issues of health care. In H. Thomae & G. L. Maddox (Eds.), *New perspectives on old age. A message to decision makers. On behalf of the international association of gerontology* (pp. 31). New York: Springer.

Tibblin, G. (1967). High blood pressure in men aged 50—A population study of men born in 1913. *Acta Med. Scand.* (Suppl. 470).

Zetterberg, C., & Andersson, G. B. J. (1982). Fractures of the proximal end of the femur in Göteborg, Sweden, 1940–1979. *Acta Ortop. Scand, 53,* 419.

3

Age, Competence, Creativity, and Wisdom

James E. Birren

The changing age structure of developed countries presents us with a demographic imperative and I call it imperative because it has a major impact on all social institutions. The simultaneous fall in birth rates and increase in life expectancy have magnified greatly the proportion of older persons in our societies. In the United States, the percentage of persons over 65 has risen from 8.2 percent in 1950 to 11.2 percent in 1980.

Some journalists regret this fact; they regard the maturing of societies as having a negative impact upon culture and economy. Such attitudes are consistent with equating productivity with physical vitality. In the recent past, leadership roles in American industry tended to be assigned to younger, middle-aged individuals, in the belief that such persons had the necessary vigor and decisiveness for those positions.

This attitude has led us, when confronted with increasing unemployment provoked by recession and technological efficiency, to retire people earlier. But this paradox of living longer and working shorter is not economically sound. The burden of even larger pensions cannot be borne indefinitely by a younger population, nor do earlier retirement policies make sense for societies or individuals. Societies cannot afford to waste the productive capacity of their older adults. Neither should societies or the elderly accept the costly and damaging insult of diminished roles and increased dependency.

My message is that our assumptions about the incapacity of older people are unsound. For people who have reasonably good health, there appears to be no negative relationship between age and productivity in our technological age, where productivity depends upon abstract skills rather than physical strength and endurance. Indeed, when characteristics of older executives are compared to those of young, rapidly rising managers, older persons in employment show not only lower absenteeism and lower accident rates, but also greater institutional loyalty. Worker attitudes best described as "I only work here; I have no feeling of pride in the job" are more characteristic of younger than older workers. The meaning of work changes with age; the intangible aspects of a job become increasingly important to the older person. Symbolic aspects of work and friendships associated with the role become important with the passage of time. Thus, the older worker and older executive are more involved in work as an institution and in the social processes that underlie it.

What is the theoretical framework behind these observations? There is perhaps no more fundamental issue in the life sciences than the nature of human aging. Clearly, research on aging at the applied and basic levels should be given a high priority in all developed countries, as we need to understand the facts about the relationship between age and productivity and the untapped potentials in older populations.

Not all aspects of individuals are in close synchrony as they age. One person may be declining physically in the later years while he may be growing psychologically. We can distinguish three ways in which humans grow old: biologically, socially, and psychologically.

First, the *biological age* of individuals refers to their position with respect to their potential lifespan; that is, their biological age is related to the probability of survival. Clearly, one can be older or younger, biologically, than one's chronological age. The measurement of the biological age of individuals includes measurements of the capacities of life-limiting organ systems. A person with a younger biological age has a longer life expectancy.

Second, the *social age* of individuals refers to their roles and social habits in comparison with other persons in a society. The question may be asked, Does an individual behave as if he were younger or older than one expects at his chronological age? Sociologists have pointed out that societies are age graded in ways of which we ordinarily are not aware. Age grading is tied to the norms and values of a particular society.

Third, the *psychological age* of individuals refers to their adaptive capacities, that is, how they adapt to changing environmental demands in terms of skills, capacities for learning, feelings, and emotions.

As we look around us we clearly can see people who are younger and older biologically, socially, and psychologically. Curiosity and intellectual vigor frequently exist within a fragile body. Still we feel that there ought to be a harmonious relationship among the three. Magnificent are those mature individuals who are biologically vigorous, socially active and productive, and who show characteristics of flexibility of mind and curiosity!

If there are three types of age—biological, social, and psychological—then there should be three types of forces moving the individual through the course of life—senescing, eldering, and geronting.

The biological processes of aging can be termed *senescing*. Senescing refers to those biological changes in the organism that render it more vulnerable, more likely to die with the passage of time. Senescing implies that, with the passage of time, the organism has a gradually lowered capacity for biological repair. Senescing is thought perhaps to depend upon a cluster of interrelated changes of a biological character rather than a single dominant factor that brings about biological vulnerability. Senescing represents our evolutionary background as a species as well as the expression of our unique heredity. The expression of our genetic endowment is the process of senescing.

The social processes of aging can be termed *eldering*. Societies vary in the extent to which they grade their roles and tasks; the process of eldering, therefore, is somewhat different across cultures and societies. Our genetic endowment is always expressed in a particular environment. Thus, the social structures of the society in which we grow up and grow old influence and limit the way we age.

The psychological process of aging can be termed *geronting*. Each individual, interacting with her genetic background and her sociocultural environment, makes choices and decisions based upon her perception of the requirements of the environment. In this sense the individual "geronts" by influencing the environment in which she will function. Individuals vary in the extent to which they have the capacity for manipulating the environment and optimizing the quality of life.

Theories of aging vary in the extent to which they emphasize the biological processes of senescing, or look at the processes of eldering that reflect the influences of the social institutions in which we grow up, or give emphasis to the choices made by individuals. Thus, there are three types of theory about aging, categorized according to what they are trying to explain:

1. *Biological theories* attempt to explain why, as we grow older, we are less likely to survive. Biological theories tend to invoke principles of molecular biology and biochemistry in genetics.

2. *Social and anthropological theories* of aging examine the position of individuals in relation to their age, as they function within a particular culture.

3. *Psychological theories* of aging address the capacities of individuals and how these capacities are exercised and employed in responding to environmental pressures or changes. Issues of concern in psychological theories are, for example, the relative passivity or activity in the individual as a force in shaping his or her life.

Unlike other biological organisms, humans have evolved with a large capacity for unique adaptations to environmental demands. The evolution of a large neocortex in the brain apparently is related to our capacity for programming ourselves on the basis of experience rather than exclusively on the basis of our genetic endowment. The term *competence* is used to refer to the effectiveness of an individual as he makes responses to environmental demands. While the social scientist emphasizes social roles, the psychologist emphasizes the blend of factors that go into competence, such as experience, skills, personality, and intellectual abilities. Unlike the narrower concept of intelligence, competence implies an environmental context for the performance of the individual. Thus, with regard to the effectiveness of adults, one is less interested in the concept of intelligence as it may predict school success than in the issues of competence and how they may vary over the course of life.

Psychological research in aging over the last 50 years has been principally concerned with intelligence and intellectual abilities. More recently interest has shifted from the measurement of intellectual abilities by standardized tests to experimental studies of cognitive processes. Generally, the evidence indicates that the normally aging adult shows a continuing rise in stored information. Some investigators label this component "crystallized intelligence." In contrast, declines are noted in "fluid intelligence" or the more dynamic aspects of perception. While considerable attention has been devoted to the differences between results from longitudinal and cross-sectional studies, the finding of some increment in crystallized intelligence is typical of most studies. This suggests that the normal brain continues to acquire stored information over the lifespan. Loss of information with age, on the other hand, is an indicator of change in health status.

Insofar as studies of intellectual abilities have been extended to learning tasks and problem solving, longitudinal findings indicate that the size of age differences or declines found in longitudinal studies are related to the type of material and the circumstances under which it is presented to the subjects.

Recent emphasis in the theory of intellectual abilities and age changes is breaking away from the earlier traditions of research in child development; that is, there is now a differential theory beginning to take into account the findings on the mature adult. Such theoretical excursions are emphasizing the change in speed of information processing or speed of behavior with age and the role of health as a factor affecting differential individual performance with age.

Generally speaking, research results indicate that health is a much bigger determinant of intellectual abilities over the lifespan than is age per se. Educational level is also a more significant factor in intellectual ability than is age. Health change is not necessarily continuous in adults; precipitous changes in intellectual abilities can be brought about in a short period of time by terminal disease or the onset of some chronic deteriorative process.

Research investigations that have begun to include larger numbers of very old individuals have shown that individuals over the age of 100 can be highly competent and effective in their performance of intellectual tasks. Given good health, individuals over the age of 100 are capable of living independently and maintaining normal interpersonal relationships. So we must differentiate further the patterns of normal change in adult life and the influence of disease.

Research is doing more than merely measuring component intellectual abilities; study is under way on how these component abilities are orchestrated or used by individuals in effective living. Thinking may be separated into convergent and divergent processes. Convergent thinking is directed to finding one and only one correct answer to a question. In contrast, divergent thought seeks different solutions or answers. In a real-life situation one often has to think of alternative uses for an object. Thus, one may think of many uses for an object like a brick or a barrel. The process of divergent thinking is not unlike having hunches in everyday life, or forming hypotheses in science. In this process, one attempts to generate alternative explanations. People good at convergent thinking are not necessarily good at divergent thinking. Apparently, the most flexible, productive minds can alternate between a divergent and convergent set of mind, depending upon the needs of the environment.

Research indicates that, during the years of employment, intelligence may not change with age in the sense of convergent thinking, but divergent thinking may decline, for reasons that need further study. Perhaps with increasing age individuals become less flexible in their modes of address to problem-solving tasks. Alternatively, divergent thinking may become extinguished by overlearning, greater dependency upon redundancy, or anxiety.

The characteristic shown by some older adults, popularly called "wisdom," is difficult to define and measure. Because of the complexities implied by the process of wisdom, most experimental psychologists avoid the topic, yet when queried about individual colleagues they may be able to attribute the trait of wisdom differentially to individuals they know.

Generally, we are more willing to attribute the quality of wisdom to individuals we favor rather than those we dislike. However, several aspects of wisdom have been isolated in addition to the common one of increased experience. Reflectiveness appears to be an attribute of wisdom, meaning that the individual acts less impulsively and is more concerned with the review of relevant information. In addition, a mastery over emotional responses seems to be associated with wisdom; thus forbearance, a wealth of experience, a familiarity with cultural background and what decisions are acceptable, and a capacity for divergent thinking all characterize the wise person. The wise person, in addition to showing forbearance and reflectiveness, must be able to come up with a novel solution.

The wise elderly person would seem to be a transcendent person, someone who effectively can overcome personal limitations and the limitations of the environment. It is not unreasonable to attribute to wise older persons the quality of transcendency; that is, they can overcome difficulties and maximize their productivity, even in the face of physical limitations. In other words, transcendent individuals go beyond physical limitations; moreover, their competence or performance cannot be judged merely from the measurement of component abilities and capacities.

While there are many dependent elderly persons whose disabilities include deficits in health, income, housing, and perhaps social networks, there are many who show late-life growth and, indeed, seek personal growth. Research has indicated three factors that contribute to the quality of later life:

1. The *pragmatics* of health, income, and housing
2. Opportunities for *contacts* with friends and family and for socialization
3. Opportunities for *growth* and creative expression of component abilities.

The transcendent elderly person is offered as a positive model for both elderly and young adults, in contrast to dependent and debilitated elderly who are preoccupied with such practical matters as money and health.

(The qualities of wisdom are sorely needed in leadership positions in various institutions of society. The use of wise elders in institutional roles is arousing interest not only because of the shift in age structure of society, but because older wise persons may bring to organizations and nations better balance and a greater capacity for dealing with long-range issues, in contrast to the immediate returns that often are of more consequence to the young.)

The question often is asked, What good is it to be old? Two sets of answers might be offered. One has to do with the benefit to the individual who is old, and the other has to do with the benefit to the family and society.

Being old must offer some advantages; otherwise why do so few people want to go back to the time when they were young? Autobiographies seem to suggest that the best time is almost always now, that much has been lived through, and the clarity of hindsight reveals the groping naiveté of younger years. There is something about experience which suggests that, however vigorous the adolescent might appear, the uncertainty of the formative years is not the peak from which we have slid downhill.

In the later years we have met our responsibilities for career, family, and community and can be free in a new sense to act with impunity. What a great sense of relief to be oneself in the later years, with less need to pose and editorialize! If used, this late-life freedom can be an introduction to an experimental phase, to pick up set-aside goals in avocation and new learning, and to pursue personal relationships that need time and energy to enjoy. Making sense out of life is certainly an inviting opportunity, especially if there are others with whom to share the evolving experience.

Society also can use those who are old. One of the common weak links in our society is the emotional bridge in families, that between children and parents. The role of surrogate parent, providing emotional stability to the young of all ages, may come naturally to many older adults. Living through many crises provides a confidence to the young that they too can "make it;" the storms of youth can be cleared by the warmth of an older, wiser head. Some of this can go on indirectly, by telling stories of the past, stories that have a point communicated by metaphor. The qualities of youth—proneness to action, vigor, decisiveness, and quickness to respond to the call of Venus—are contrasted to the qualities of old age—stability, experience, and the detachment of wisdom.

If statesmen were wise we would not need youth to spend itself in battle. Old age not only symbolizes qualities that younger persons wish to possess; it has real qualities than can help the young to grow more than old.

4

The Mystique of Age

Betty Friedan

In the last 20 years I have journeyed from the confrontation with what I called the feminine mystique to my current confrontation with the mystique of age. I now am applying the lessons of 20 years spent articulating a new direction and redefinition of the role of women, to addressing our negative, dependent stereotypes about age. My authority comes as a participant/observer of the greatest movement of social change of this time, the women's movement. That experience gives me perspective at the verge of what I think will be the greatest movement of social change of the last decades of this century: Breaking through the mystique of age to the personhood of age. The analogies between the two movements are not perfect, but they are illuminating.

The image of woman in the United States, in the years after World War II up through the 1950s and into the 1960s, was only in sexual relation to man: Woman defined as a housewife, as mother, as the server of the physical needs of husband, children, and home; woman defined not as a person or by her own actions in society. This was the only image of women in the mass media, denying the reality of increasing numbers of women who were working outside the home. This image was imbedded in psychological and sociological thought. Indeed, it re-invoked images of women imbedded in the Judeo-Christian tradition, in religion, in old prejudices—woman as child, woman as something not quite human—and gave these images an honored place in sophisticated scholarship, Freudian doctrine, and sociological function.

So, even those who treated women's ills and problems—and there was increasing talk about the woman problem, just as there's talk today about the aging problem—defined the problem in terms of that image: Why are all these American women so frustrated and depressed in their role as woman? Why aren't they fulfilled in their role as woman? Is it education that is making them frustrated in their role as woman?

Women were immersed in guilt if they didn't quite fit the prevailing image. They had a problem, as I was beginning to hear from women, that didn't have to do with their marriage, their children, or their sexuality, but had to do with needs to move in society, yearnings to be a person. "I'm my husband's wife, I'm my children's mother, I'm a server of meals and a cleaner of diapers and a service station for others, but who am I for myself?" It was a problem that had no name. There was no name from any of the experts for problems having to do with the personhood of woman, woman's need to grow and participate in society.

Of course, after World War II a lot of us were at home having children and backyard barbecues, living the American Dream, the dream of the world. We had a lovely house with a dishwasher and a washing machine and carpeting and a station wagon and a husband who was supposed to take care of us. Women in America, even educated women, were marrying younger and younger and were giving up their own education to put their husbands through college, because education suddenly was no longer considered so important for women. Career had become a dirty word because a woman's fulfillment was not as a person, but through marriage. She had children, she had a house, but she wasn't satisfied.

Only women felt this way. To try and understand why, I looked in the psychology books, for I was trained as a psychologist and I had been through Freudian analysis. The problem had no name. Something strange was going on here. I was an established magazine writer, but none of the magazines would print my description of this pervasive problem. Each time I was turned down I did more research. I got more interviews, talked to more experts, and was more and more sure that something very bad was going on: What was bad was what everybody else thought was good, and the problem wasn't what everybody said the problem was at all.

I suddenly realized I couldn't get it into print, because the very magazines I was writing for and the places where I was looking for answers were permeated by the image that was creating the problem in the first place. So, I called it the feminine mystique, because I was beginning to be aware that it was not a reality. In fact, it was distorting reality, thereby causing problems and keeping women from recognizing what their real problems were.

So, I wrote a book called *The Feminine Mystique*, based on what I was hearing from women themselves, questioning the assumptions of this image, asking how it came about and what was keeping it intact when, in fact, it denied the reality of women's life.

Bringing the mystique to consciousness was crucial. A mystique can't be defined; it is half-unconscious, a miasma, a congruence of images that we accept as reality. I prefer mystique to stereotype, because it conveys emotional reality. We think it's real. We think it's true. We call it mystique only when we understand that it is a distortion, a denial of reality. For instance, the image of woman solely in terms of her biological role as mother was not a mystique in biblical times. It was not a mystique several hundred years ago. It was basically true. But it became a mystique when it came to deny the reality of women now and the challenge they face in modern society. Breaking through the feminine mystique and taking ourselves seriously as persons is what the women's movement is really all about. Recognizing the personhood of woman enables us to see differently the problems in our own lives and ultimately to see differently the problems of woman in society. The problem was not why women weren't adjusted in their role solely as housewives and mothers but why they weren't moving in society as full people.

So I looked for patterns beyond the feminine mystique, but there were no patterns, because the women my own age and younger were still in the postwar baby boom and living the feminine mystique, and the few women who were deviating from it were more or less guiltily coping with their own problems, alone. The women who were combining jobs and professions with marriage and motherhood out of choice, not just necessity, were older. They looked different from the frustrated suburban housewives I'd been interviewing. There was vitality in them. Their very skin looked different. I began asking them about their menopause. They hadn't had it. "What do you mean you haven't had the menopause?" I would ask, for they were in their fifties, after all. Their menses had, in fact, stopped; they just didn't remember when. They hadn't had menopause in the traumatic way menopause was supposed to occur. The menopause in America and elsewhere, I think, was considered the end of a woman's life, really.

There were just some leftover years to live. In the mental hospitals in the United States, one of the prime diagnostic categories along with *senile dementia* was *involutional melancholia,* a psychosis that had been considered virtually normal for women in menopause and afterwards, a state of extreme depression. But these older women whom I was interviewing didn't have depression; they didn't have the menopause in that sense. I couldn't understand it. I went around talking to some of the experts on menopause, and there were no explanations.

That was my first sense of something new happening with women and age. Does something happen to the aging process when women move beyond that previous biological definition of the female sex role to larger human purposes, a larger definition of personhood?

Then I put that question on the back burner as I myself moved to organizing the women's movement. Women in general in America were beginning to see that it wasn't enough to say, "I am a person." We had to change society. We had to break through sex discrimination. There was not even a word for sex discrimination or sexism then. We had to demand our equal rights and opportunities as women, and we needed a social movement to do so. We empowered ourselves in each other. I cannot believe now how powerless women were thought to be and thought themselves to be at that time, only 20 years ago.

In the 20 years since then, the whole image of woman and the definition of the woman problem have changed. Women are no longer "a problem" for society; women are posing problems. They are solving their own problems, they use laws, they use court cases, they challenge and have begun to break through the stereotype of women as passive, dreary housewives. We see many and various active images of women in television now and, above all, in life. There is a wonderful emergence of role models for the new woman, a sense of great growth and the potential of woman's creativity. Women are confronting their personhood and beginning to have their own voice in all fields and professions.

About five years ago, Robert Butler called me up and asked me to come to see him in Washington. He was head of the National Institute on Aging, and he said, "I want you to get interested in aging, because," he said, "the policies and the research on aging in America are formulated mostly by men, based on the lives of men and the experience of men, but most of the aged are women."

Now, I wasn't a bit interested in aging. My life had begun anew, as had many women's lives in America at age 35 or 40 or 45. Aging seemed dreary, remote, almost unthinkable. But I remembered the observations I had made of some changes in the aging process of women. Come to think of it, I had menopause myself somewhere back then in the midst of the women's movement, after *The Feminine Mystique*, but I can't remember when. By now the change that I had seen only in a few women was absolutely epidemic in society. By now millions of women, who were supposed to decline and get ready for death after menopause, were back in colleges, universities, going to work, marching, talking back to male chauvinists, revolutionizing home life, revolutionizing concepts of sexuality, demanding to be preachers and rabbis and priests, moving into space as astronauts. No longer were women 3 percent of the students in medical school and law school; they were 35 percent. And many of these wonderful, vibrant new women were over 45. The whole picture of aging for women was changing.

Now I began to worry about men. It had become clear that there was an enormous discrepancy between the life expectancy of women and men, and it was getting worse and worse. I had also begun to wonder how far women could go just by themselves. A lot of these vibrant women were complaining that there were no men. Men seemed to be stuck in dreary routines. They were tired, rigid, up-tight, threatened, and, if they were my age, they often were dead. Something must be seriously wrong with the role of men. If menopause was no longer traumatic for women, why were there now all these new traumas of the male midlife crisis? Why were men dying so young?

Robert Butler said, "I can't answer those questions from research yet; in fact most of the researchers aren't even asking those questions." So I went home and a Geiger counter started clicking in my mind, and I knew that examining aging was the next direction in my life. Five years ago I turned another corner and began my own search into what this breakthrough in aging for women really meant, and what it might mean for men. I applied for grants from the Ford Foundation and the National Endowment for the Humanities, and I got them. And then people began to say to me, "Oh, you are working on a book about aging," and their eyes would glaze over. I would say, "No, no, no, I'm not working on a book about aging. I've got some far-out hypotheses about women, men, and the aging process, but I'm not working on a book about aging." I didn't know why, but I felt this terrible dread of doing a book about aging.

So I decided instead to write a book about the second stage of the women's movement. I sensed that, while we had to do what we did, we couldn't really come to full terms with the personhood of woman using the male model. We had to have a new model encompassing female experiences and values. The second stage couldn't be done in terms of women alone; it had to be done in terms of men, too. We had to restructure society. I had to write that book, really, before I could immerse myself in the book I am now writing, called *The Fountain of Age*.

I hit my own sixtieth birthday at this time, and I guess I began to confront my own denial of age. It was then that I came to full confrontation with the mystique of age. I experienced a strange *déjà vu* as, at Harvard and at meetings of gerontological associations, I immersed myself in the state of the art: geriatrics and gerontology. I had a sense that experts on aging—clinicians, counselors, researchers—were treating "the problem of age" in the same kind of patronizing (and compassionate) tones that I had heard 20 years ago from the experts on women. Somehow, they were denying the personhood of aging people. The only work at Harvard on aging was being done at the medical school, mainly research on senility, particularly Alzheimer's disease, and some abstract policy research into the care of the elderly in nursing homes and hospitals. And yet only 5 percent of Americans are in nursing homes; only 20 percent will ever be in nursing homes in their lives. Only 4 percent of Americans will suffer from senile dementia of the Alzheimer's type, and only another 10 percent have any kind of senility. Yet the experts—the gerontologists and the geriatricians—were dealing primarily with age in terms of senility and nursing homes. The media were beginning to report about "the problem of age" in the same way that 20 years earlier they had started talking about "the woman problem." And the problem of age was: How is society going to deal with these infirm, senile, helpless, passive, defenseless, dependent, sick crocks?

There is an age mystique just as there was a feminine mystique, and it too frustrates and depresses elderly people by diminishing their self-esteem and their expectations for themselves. The mystique of age is, I believe, built into many professions and into professional training. Despite my work on the feminine mystique and in the women's movement, only now can I confront my own denial of age and come to concrete personal terms with it—not the abstract "problem of age," not "them," those dreary aging men and women, so remote from the vital reality of you and me. Now I can say "I." I am 62 years old. I am myself, at 62. I am not that different from who I was at 61, at 60, at 45. I don't feel the way I'm supposed to feel at 62. I don't act as I'm supposed to act at 62. I am myself. I am going to listen to myself.

Why is there such a schizophrenic split between the dreary image of age and the vital reality of the women and men in their sixties, seventies, and eighties; people whom I am interviewing now, wherever I can find them; men and women pursuing new directions in or beyond profession, from a great artist moving to a new stage in his seventies to a housewife finding her own identity after widowhood? Someone hears about my work and says, "You've got to meet my mother. She came alive at 70. She was a saleswoman in the Children's Department at Bloomingdale's. She was supposed to quit, but they kept her on and now she runs the whole department. She's 82." Such people don't even fit *my* image of age, so dramatic is the vital reality of this person who is 82, this person who is 91, this person who is 73 or 68. I say, "You don't look that old, you look much younger than 82 or 68." They can't *all* be that exceptional, but they all *are* very different from the mystique of age that has structured our perceptions and discussions.

Just as we did with the feminine mystique, we must examine the mystique of age to be able to develop an image of age that is not completely negative. For the mystique of age that permeates the mass media is shared by commissions, researchers, gerontologists, and geriatricians, as well as aging people themselves—the image of age as childlike, dependent, passive, sick, mindless, and senile.

A study was done at Harvard in which people from three different age groups—young, middle-aged, and older—were asked to diagnose certain problems in these two situations: (1) when the person with the problem is described as young and (2) when the person with the same problem is described as old. Young and middle-aged people tended to see older people—people over 60—primarily as alone, passive, or senile, as sick and dependent; whereas older people themselves tended to see older people as engaged in activity with others and as independent people. But people who were going from middle age to old age themselves were more likely to see forgetfulness in others, which a younger person would simply characterize as "he forgot," in extremely negative terms, as senility. It's a distancing mechanism, as if to say, "*I* am never going to be like that."

We associate age with disease. Even gerontologists or geriatricians concentrate on the most negative aspects of aging, which Butler and Birren and Svanborg show are pathologies of aging, not the norms of aging at all. To limit discussion of aging to the negative norms of aging ignores the growth that so often accompanies aging. Pathologies are what we think of as aging, even when we say we are going to study normal aging, because we distance ourselves that way.

We must come to grips with this mystique of age just as we did with the feminine mystique. Unless we break through the age mystique, we endlessly ruminate on the problem, How can we deal with this mass of unproductive people? How can our productivity somehow encompass or support so many passive, dependent people? That's the way the problem is being defined in the United States, where suddenly Social Security is seen as being in crisis because of demographics. As the number of people living past 60, 70, and 80 increases, their very existence is seen as the problem. We have to reformulate our thinking. How do we develop and use our human potential in age as a part of a productive society?

We are kept from doing so by the barriers in the structure of employment, the barriers of age discrimination, the barriers in our own and others' expectations, in environments that do not challenge—indeed, restrict—that potential of vital human aging, the barriers of expected disease or dependency.

There's a breath of fresh air when we suddenly stop dealing with the aged as crocks and deal with them as people who might be productive. We must do so not just out of compassion toward the aged; we must do so out of a need to involve their skills and their wisdom in enriching our whole society. We must celebrate the personhood of age. We must confront the reality that in age individuation reaches its zenith. Individual differences in every aspect of behavior and personality are greatest in age. Constraints of biology matter less in this third age, for research shows there is more individual difference in age than anywhere else. Individuation—except when there's an extreme deprivation through poverty or induced passivity, induced dependency, induced helplessness—can reach a greater peak and does reach a greater range in the third age. Freed in age from certain constraints of biology or role that previously imposed on the personality, personhood can emerge as a precious theme in this new period of life, just as personhood has emerged for women in the last 20 years.

5

Working Past Retirement: Practical and Motivational Issues

Maurice Lazarus
Harvey Lauer

One of the most profound demographic trends of the twentieth century is the increase in human longevity and the corollary growth of the elderly population. At the turn of the century, only 40 percent of people born survived until the age of 65. Today, a full 75 percent live to be 65 or more, and once people reach 65 their longevity continues to improve. In 1900, life expectancy at age 65 was 11 years; by 1980 it had increased to 16 years. In just three decades (1950 to 1980) the over-65 population has doubled. During the same period, the number of Americans over 80 has *tripled*.

In contrast to this growth of the elderly population is the countertrend toward early male retirement. In 1950, 86 percent of all American men 55 to 64 were in the labor force; by 1980 the number had decreased to 71 percent. For men over 65 the drop in labor-force participation was far more dramatic, from 42 percent to 18 percent. If this countertrend continues, the economic and social consequences for society will be far reaching. For individuals, the psychological impact is inestimable. For society, the macroeconomic implications of a diminishing elderly labor force range far beyond the present beleaguered American Social Security system. In 1950, there were eight workers aged 18 to 64 for each worker over 65. By 1980, the ratio had fallen to 5 to 1. In the year 2030, when the baby boom generation enters retirement age, there will be only three workers to support each worker over 65.

In addition to the economic tensions inherent in such a scenario, there exists a very real potential for social strain and intergenerational conflict. Several "redistributive" solutions have been proposed for the retirement dilemma. Among them are an increase in the income taxes of workers; raising Social Security taxes; reducing Social Security benefits; or taxing Social Security benefits as income. A more equitable and compelling solution is the *reversal* of the trend toward early retirement through the creation of job opportunities for older workers. Not only is this an economic imperative for American society, but a psychological imperative as well.

For many people, retirement now lasts as long as the period of childhood and adolescence. Not only has longevity increased, but so has the span over which a majority of Americans remain physically and intellectually vigorous. We need, therefore, to find out how those extra years of life can be enhanced and how the skills and experience of this growing segment of the population can be mobilized to benefit the community. In particular, we need to reevaluate our assumptions about elderly Americans in the workplace.

The increase in life expectancy and good health is of little benefit to people who are denied the self-esteem and fulfillment derived from satisfying and meaningful activities. More often than not, these needs are bound up with some form of institutionalized work. The effects of compulsory retirement are portrayed in a report by the American Medical Association Committee on Aging:

> This condition—enforced idleness—robs those affected of the will to live full, well-rounded lives, deprives them of opportunities for compelling physical and mental activity, and encourages atrophy and decay. It robs the worker of his initiative and independence. It narrows physical and mental horizons. Compulsory retirement on the basis of age will impair the health of many individuals whose job represents a major source of status, creative satisfaction, social relationships or self-respect.

Idleness and isolation are linked with increased incidence of neuroses, obesity, alcoholism, and a host of other maladies. Indeed, the highest incidence of suicide for white males occurs in the 70-and-over age group. People over 65 need and want to remain active. A study of 1200 people who had lived to be 100 years old concluded that "usefulness" and "work" remained the most consistently accurate of all the factors predicting survival to a very old age. One subject in this study was quoted as saying, "Man must work. I think we have to begin by realizing that work is a biological necessity."

ATTITUDES TOWARD RETIREMENT

In the 1979 Harris study titled "1979 Study of American Attitudes towards Pensions and Retirement" (Harris, 1979), nearly half of all retirees (46%) indicated that they would prefer to be working. For those over 65 and still working, economic need was not an important reason. In an earlier Harris study (1974), 10 percent of the elderly sample—over 2 million people—expressed a desire to volunteer their services. This is in addition to the 4.6 million elderly who already do some form of volunteer work.

Of almost 8000 respondents in the Retirement History Study, 86 percent stated that they considered work as one of the most meaningful parts of life. More important perhaps was the finding that the vast majority of older people (84%) also believe that "others think more highly of those who work."

In a 1982 survey of the American workforce by the Public Agenda Foundation, less than half of workers over 55 (48%) claimed that money was a reason for their desire to work past retirement. Psychological factors were much more important: the need to keep busy (83%), enjoyment of work (92%), the chance to mix with people (83%), and the desire to use one's skills and experience (77%). In the same study, remarkably strong relationships existed between the level of "psychic" income derived from one's job and preference for working past 65. This phenomenon will be discussed later.

If so many older people recognize the psychological benefits of remaining active and express a desire to continue working, why then do we find only a relative handful of workers over 65 in the labor force?

In 1982, labor-force participation rates for people over 65 was 12 percent. This is in stark contrast to the 52 percent of workers over 55 who, in the 1982 Public Agenda Foundation survey, expressed a desire to continue some form of paid work after 65. A nationwide panel survey, the Retirement History Study, gave some indication of the volatility of retirement attitudes. Generally, about half of all workers interviewed said that they intended to retire at 65. Many of these workers may have preferred to stay on in some capacity past the age of 65 but for various reasons decided in advance that it was not practical to do so. When interviewed four years later, after they had passed the retirement age, most had in fact retired. The gap between people's attitudes about retirement and subsequent behavior becomes evident in the retirement histories of the other half of the sample—those respondents who expected to work past 65. Four years after the initial survey, a full 40 percent of those who "never expected to retire" had indeed joined the ranks of the superannuated.

Obstacles to Productivity

There obviously are several major obstacles in the path of those who wish to work past 65.

1. First, there is poor health. Older Americans, according to self-assessments, are healthier than ever. In 1972, 49 percent of those over 65 described their health as either "good" or "excellent"; in 1980, the figure had climbed to 60 percent. Still, a 1981 Harris poll revealed that more than one retiree in three (37%) had been compelled to retire due to poor health or disability. It should be noted that, while poor health is a major deterrent to a longer work life, it is probably not a major explanation of the gap between people's attitudes and their behavior toward retirement. This is because poor health usually influences one's original preference for retirement; that is, poor health will cause people to opt for retirement in the first place; most people don't "discover" (after making a decision to work) that ill health or disability will prevent them from working.

2. The financial disincentives to continued participation in the labor force are well known. Increases in Social Security benefits, the earnings limitation on Social Security recipients, the availability of private pensions, and other financially attractive early retirement incentives all militate against working past the age of 65.

3. The majority of people over 65 who want to work would prefer part-time employment. Many would like flexible schedules or less traditional work arrangements such as job sharing or the opportunity

to work at home. However, a sufficient number of such jobs simply do not exist, and the competition for such jobs is becoming more intense.

4. Technological change plays a role too. Opportunities for older workers may be further impeded by new layers of structural unemployment resulting from technological job elimination. These structural changes in the labor market may further intensify the jobs competition between the generations. For this reason, the concept of volunteerism, discussed in a later section, may assume a new importance.

But even if all the obstacles and disincentives to employment were removed and sufficient job opportunities were created, how effective would our new army of older workers be?

Opportunities for older workers seem to be shrouded by myths and stereotypes. Not only do such misperceptions impede opportunities for paid work, they also establish inferior standards for the organization of volunteer efforts. Among the most common caricatures of the older worker are a lack of mental and physical stamina, a resistance to change, higher absenteeism, lower productivity, and a decided aversion to new ideas and creative enterprises. As a result of these stereotypes, even the best-intentioned corporate job creation initiatives or volunteerism philosophies are built upon a foundation of patronage. Consequently, job creation programs in both the paid and unpaid sectors often assume a "secondary" character, dominated by a philosophy of "light," undemanding jobs such as tour guides, messengers, or varieties of "go-for" jobs which often do not maximize the full potential of older workers.

Older workers are different from younger ones, but those differences are found on both sides of the work performance ledger. There is no question that physical powers eventually diminish with age. There is also much research to suggest that adults tend to be more cautious as they grow older. While older people may be slower at some tasks, they may be better problem solvers in other areas. They may be less able to deal with large amounts of complex data than their younger counterparts. They also may be slower decision makers, but they may be right more often. In some cases, workers over 65 have the best peformance record of any age group (U.S. Department of Labor, 1965). Older workers, especially those over 65, are much less likely to suffer occupational injuries than younger ones

TABLE 5.1.   Retirement preferences by collar and education

	Total %	White Collar %	Blue Collar %	H.S. or Less %	Coll. Grad. %
Would prefer to stop work at 65 or sooner	47	43	52	54	34
Would prefer to continue working past 65	47	51	42	42	60
Not Sure/Don't Know	6	6	6	4	6
	100	100	100	100	100

Source: Data from Public Agenda Foundation, National Survey (1982).

(Root, 1981). And older workers are not only capable of benefiting from on-the-job training, they are more likely to complete the training and remain with their employer upon completion than younger workers (Sheppard & Rix, 1977). Perhaps the most important consideration is one that is related to the question of older-worker capability: In most jobs, a worker's capacity to perform far exceeds the demands of the job.

Physical Demands of Jobs

The 1982 survey by the Public Agenda Foundation revealed that 52 percent of all blue-collar workers said that they wanted to retire at or before 65, versus only 43 percent for white-collar workers (see Table 5.1). It has been universally assumed that this modest but significant difference can be explained in terms of the more strenuous and taxing nature of blue-collar jobs. But once again, the conventional wisdom is wide of the mark. Among blue-collar workers, the perception of one's job as "strenuous" does not distinguish between those who would like to retire at 65 from those who would prefer to continue working. Important considerations in opting to continue working past 65 for blue-collar workers are opportunities to be creative, to do interesting work, and to see the end results of one's work. Indeed, the difference in retirement preferences among white- and blue-collar workers of *all ages* is far better explained as a function of work gratification (see

TABLE 5.2.   Job characteristics, collar, and retirement preferences

"Describes Job Fully"	White Collar		Blue Collar	
	Retire %	Work %	Retire %	Work %
Have a great deal of discretion as to how hard I work	53	54	33	47
Job allows me to be creative	36	45	18	36
Job challenges me to do my best	54	57	42	53
Can see end results of my work	57	60	45	59
A great deal of responsibility	56	69	51	54
Have the opportunity to develop my abilities and potential	44	54	31	34
"Suited" for present occupation	73	88	66	73
Interesting work	58	72	41	53
Can learn new things	46	59	34	44

Source: Data from Public Agenda Foundation, National Survey (1982).

Table 5.2). For older workers, the patterns were similar to the responses of blue-collar workers in that physically taxing jobs did not deter respondents over 55 from stating that they would like to continue working past age 65 (see Table 5.3). In sum, these data clearly suggest that, for older workers (as well as for workers in general), retirement preferences are affected little by the physical demands of a job, but can be influenced greatly by the psychic gratification derived therein.

Resistance to Change

Perhaps one of the better tests of people's receptivity to new ideas and changes is to examine their attitudes toward the introduction of new technology. In the 1982 Public Agenda Foundation study, workers over 55 were just as prone as their younger counterparts to approve of the introduction of new technology and to state that new technology will make jobs more interesting and challenging. In fact, more than half of the over-55 group who already had experienced

TABLE 5.3.   Job characteristics and retirement preferences of older workers

"Describes Job Fully"	Workers over 55 prefer to:	
	Retire %	Work %
Job allows me to be creative	24	47
Can see end results of my work	41	62
Have a chance to develop abilities and potential	38	53
Job challenges me to do my best	56	58
Interesting work	58	64
Recognition for good work	45	45
Work for people who treat me with respect	53	57
Work with people I like	62	55
Feel like part of a team	58	62
Good fringe benefits	63	39

Source: Data from Public Agenda Foundation, National Survey (1982).

major technological changes on the job (51%) indicated that their jobs had become more interesting as a result (see Table 5.4). For workers under 55, the proportion who shared this view was only 39 percent. Workers over 55 were just as likely to endorse the values of achievement, creativity, and self-fulfillment as were the remainder of the sample (see Table 5.5).

Work Ethic

A Public Agenda Foundation study (1982) has provided a more detailed examination of what might be called the "unwritten work contract"—the assumptions made by each individual about what he or she gives to the job and expects to get in return. Respondents were presented with four alternative work "contracts." One characterized the traditional conception of the job as an essentially economic transaction where work is given in exchange for pay. A second represented another traditional view of work as an unpleasant necessity. The third represented a somewhat newer vision of work as interesting and desirable in its own right but limited in the claims it should make on a

TABLE 5.4.　Receptivity to new technology

	Total %	18–29 %	30–44 %	45–54 %	55+ %
The introduction of new technology will make jobs more interesting and challenging	69	72	68	69	68
We should introduce new technology as rapidly as possible, even if some jobs are lost	32	28	32	36	34
Worker has experienced major technological job changes	22	16	20	28	30
As a result of major technological changes, job became more interesting	41	39	41	39	51

Source: Data from Public Agenda Foundation, National Survey (1982).

TABLE 5.5.　Developmental and fulfillment needs

	Total %	18–29 %	30–44 %	45–54 %	55+ %
Would prefer a job with more interesting work vs. a job with more income	56	53	57	57	57
Work mainly to develop self as a person	17	18	17	16	18
Most important personal values:					
Self-fulfillment	43	42	43	46	41
Creativity	25	21	26	29	26
Achievement	37	35	36	39	40

Source: Data from Public Agenda Foundation, National Survey (1982).

person's energies and commitments. The fourth contract presented a strong version of the work ethic where work is deemed to have intrinsic moral value for its own sake. Those respondents who felt that the fourth contract best described their work relationships were considered to have a strong work ethic.

Those same studies show that older workers, especially those over 55, tend to have a stronger work ethic, to be more satisfied with their jobs, more committed and hardworking, and more loyal to their employers (see Table 5.6). Here are some specific findings:

TABLE 5.6.   Work attitudes

	Total	18–29	30–44	45–54	55+
	%	%	%	%	%
Have an inner need to do the very best job I can, regardless of pay	52	46	53	47	67
Exert a great deal of additional effort on the job	55	46	54	62	66
I'm committed to both my job and my employer	54	50	49	61	67
Feel a great deal of loyalty toward organization	46	37	44	52	61
Organization has a great deal of loyalty toward me	28	21	27	32	38
Need more people at my place of work	34	38	36	30	24

Source: Data from Public Agenda Foundation, National Survey (1982).

- Sixty-seven percent of workers over 55 stated that they have an inner need to do the very best job they can, regardless of pay; this view is shared by only 46 percent of the 18-to-29 group.
- Similarly, 66 percent of the over-55 sample claimed that they exerted a great deal of extra effort on the job, versus 54 percent for the 30-to-44 cohort and only 46 percent for those 18 to 29.
- Similar patterns emerged among respondents who said that they felt a great deal of loyalty toward employers: 61 percent of those over 55 felt such loyalty; figures for the other age groups were 45 to 54 (52%), 30 to 44 (44%), and 18 to 29 (37%).
- Eighty percent of all workers over 55 expressed a desire to remain on their present jobs, even if they had other options. This view was shared by 61 percent of those 45 to 54, 48 percent of the 30-to-44 age group, and only 34 percent of the 18-to-29 sample.

There is also evidence to suggest that the improvement of work attitudes with age is widespread across cultures. In an international study by the Public Agenda Foundation (1982), similar attitudinal patterns by age were found in four other countries (see Table 5.7).

Without the benefit of longitudinal data on the older age cohorts, it is impossible to speculate whether the more favorable attitudes of older workers represent a phase of the maturation process (which eventually will be shared by all age groups) or if the less-positive values of today's younger workers are an enduring manifestation of a values revolution. The message, in any event, is that older workers have a decidedly stronger work ethic and more positive attitude toward work than their younger counterparts. Given the right conditions, these attitudes and values could be mustered to form an effective pool of human resources that could fulfill the psychic needs of the older population as well as begin to address one of our most pressing economic problems.

ALTERNATIVES TO RETIREMENT

In the Public Agenda Foundation study (1982), 67 percent of those who indicated a preference for work after 65 stated that they would prefer part time work. In 1982, 48 percent of the nearly three million employed persons over 65 were engaged in part-time work. In the 1981 Harris Study, workers over 55 endorsed the following work time options as a "great deal of help" in enabling them to extend their work lives:

Part-time work (50%)
At-home work (46%)
Job-sharing (38%)
Flex-time (29%)
Full-time work (24%)
Compressed 4-day week (21%)

Unfortunately, the adoption of alternative work schedules by business and industry is still relatively limited; however, a number of corporations have already implemented a wide range of work options to encourage the retention of older workers. The major categories of these alternative arrangements are:

TABLE 5.7. Selected work attitudes and job characteristics by age. International comparisons

	Sweden			Japan			Israel		
	18–29 %	30–54 %	55+ %	18–29 %	30–54 %	55+ %	18–29 %	30–54 %	55+ %
Strong work ethic	42	44	49	36	51	58	63	54	67
Good fit between job and work values	44	53	54	27	31	36	64	53	46
Have both work ethic and good fit between job and work values	17	24	26	13	19	24	41	29	31
Work for self development	24	22	22	23	14	17	25	16	7
Participates in policy decisions	28	33	22	33	50	46	n.a.	n.a.	n.a.
Pay is less than I deserve	36	32	36	44	44	44	n.a.	n.a.	n.a.
Have "bad" job	18	14	13	18	16	19	8	6	2
Fully committed to my work	45	58	55	n.a.	n.a.	n.a.	75	81	71
Feel a great deal of loyalty to organization	27	41	51	6	25	48	n.a.	n.a.	n.a.

	U.S.A.			West Germany			United Kingdom		
	18–29 %	30–54 %	55+ %	18–29 %	30–54 %	55+ %	18–29 %	30–54 %	55+ %
Strong work ethic	44	49	69	18	25	38	13	18	21
Good fit between job and work values	43	47	48	44	46	50	6	5	7
Have both work ethic and work values	23	26	41	9	14	22	3	8	8
Work for self-development	18	16	17	18	20	21	10	9	5
Participates in policy decisions	9	17	16	n.a.	n.a.	n.a.	23	25	25
Pay is less than I deserve	n.a.	n.a.	n.a.	73	66	69	24	20	28
Have "bad" job	10	8	4	26	17	20	21	21	27
Fully committed to my work	61	70	73	32	44	58	57	69	74
Feel a great deal of loyalty to organization	37	45	59	25	30	35	n.a.	n.a.	n.a.

59

Modified work schedules
Nontraditional, part-time arrangements
Temporary employment
Redesigned jobs
Transfer or reassignment
New careers
Volunteerism

Modified Work Schedules

One of the most innovative approaches to modified work schedules exists at Kuempel Chime Clock Works, a small, privately owned manufacturing company whose entire workforce is composed of older workers. Each employee's work hours are set according to that person's needs. About half of the employees work over 20 hours a week. Those who work full time are eligible for the company's pension and insurance plan; many of the part-time workers are retired and receive Social Security. Training is informal at Kuempel. Although employees are hired for a specific task, workers often can perform several different jobs. As a result, the company is flexible when vacation time, illness, or other circumstances require shifts in work schedules. Some workers with sick spouses have been able to take home certain portable work. Accommodating workers with flexible schedules has produced an atmosphere conducive to the employment of older workers. Kuempel's personnel policies have attracted many older workers to the company.

Redesigning work schedules is also a successful option for large retail corporations. Except in the case of its executive employees, R. H. Macy & Company does not impose a mandatory retirement age; consequently, many employees have opted for an abbreviated work schedule to adjust gradually to retirement. With special permission, some first-line supervisors also have arranged to postpone their retirement by assuming a short-hour schedule.

Another example of a flexible arrangement is the one devised by Ideal Security Hardware, a company that uses older people to perform jobs that permit flexible scheduling. Some older workers file and mail on a part-time basis, and they are free to choose any four hours during the day. This company also has placed its janitorial jobs on a part-time, flex-hour basis. Although Ideal Hardware is unionized by the Teamsters, the union has not objected to the company's older-worker, flex-hour practices.

Major innovations in new job arrangements for older workers were facilitated in California with the passage of legislation that permitted part-time employees of the public schools to receive retirement payment commensurate with previous full-time work. One of the work options developed by the Board of Education of the San Francisco United School District effectively redesigned work schedules for those who wished to continue teaching on a half-time basis. Under certain conditions, teachers over 55 who had 10 years of service with the district could reduce their previous year's workload by 50 percent. Teachers who have chosen this plan have opted for a variety of schedules, including teaching full-time for half a year, teaching half a day, or alternating two- and three-day weeks.

Nontraditional Part-time Arrangements

A variation on the part-time theme is job sharing, an increasingly popular option. At the Minnesota Abstract & Title Company, a number of white-collar jobs are filled by pairs of workers, enabling many older workers to work steadily at a reduced pace. Each member of the pair works full-time for a month and then is off for a month while the other partner covers.

In Kansas, the Wichita Public School system is experimenting with a novel job-sharing program. This program is limited to the elementary level and is guided by a Board of Education policy that accepts teacher-initiated job-sharing proposals. The policy permits teachers to decide how they will divide their teaching tasks, schedule their time, and communicate with each other and the rest of the school staff. Prior to 1978, teachers participating in job sharing could receive only half of their salaries and benefits, computed on a half-time basis. More recent legislation, however, permits employees to retire at age 60 or over, to receive their pensions, and also to be guaranteed reemployment after retirement. Under this new policy, more incentives exist for job sharing. A teacher who was earning $15,000 a year now can collect a pension of $7,000, along with half a salary, for a total of $14,500. It is expected that an increase in job sharing will create fruitful teaching arrangements combining older and younger workers.

Also beneficial for both the firm and the older worker are arrangements by which employees can gain further education and/or training while remaining with the company. In Japan, for instance, many companies provide for the continuing education of older employees. Health management programs are devised to maintain the physical fitness of aging employees. One company makes available to older workers a six-month course for building physical stamina and provides adult classes in such subjects as English conversation, writing, and public speaking. Courses on store management, accounting, and appliance repair are open only to employees over 40. Partial tuition reimbursement is another educational option available for workers enrolled in work-related courses.

Among American companies, IBM has established a tuition reimbursement program for older workers. IBM's Retirement Education Assistance Plan provides potential retirees and their spouses with $2,500 each in tuition aid, beginning three years prior to retirement eligibility and ending two years after retirement. This enables older workers to develop new interests and/or prepare for a second career. For employees who wish to extend their working years through a job shift, IBM also has innovative programs. Employees of all ages have participated in IBM programs that prepare workers for their new jobs.

Atlantic Richfield, which employs 50,000 people, has its own educational policy, maintaining and paying fringe benefits for employees who choose up to two years of unpaid educational leave. While this option is open to all employees, it is particularly valuable for older workers who wish to prepare for a second career.

"Phased retirement" is oriented more toward easing the transition to retirement than it is toward extending one's working years; however, it does provide insight into the flexible work schedules that a company can adopt. Wrigley, a Chicago-based company with 6,000 employees, permits anyone who stays until the company's normal retirement age of 65 the choice of taking one month off without pay the next year, two months the following year, and three the third year, followed by full retirement at age 69. Employees are compensated for reduced income with an increased pension. Prentice-Hall has a similar concept; employees can reduce their schedule in hours per day or days per week. After a predetermined period, the employee must retire.

Temporary Employment

In addition to its part-time work option, the San Francisco Unified School District has devised an interesting consulting arrangement for older workers. Their Early Retirement Consultant Plan enables eligible teachers to retire, receive full pension, and be hired as consultants for duties other than classroom teaching. In their newly designed jobs, these former teachers may participate in a variety of capacities, including curriculum development, special studies, training of new teachers, development of organizational skills, general administration, and office work. Consultants are paid per diem and may work a set number of days, dependent upon age. Many teachers have enrolled in this popular program, which enables them to work after retirement under new circumstances and schedules.

The Sun Company, the nation's tenth largest oil company, with 35,000 employees, began experimenting with hiring annuitants on a temporary basis in early 1979. The company was immediately pleased with the overwhelming response and the quality of the annuitants' work. Robert Custer, Director of Retired Relations, reported that some hiring managers "were afraid of having little old ladies or men doddering around. But these people came in full of vigor, gave a full eight hours of work with no two-hour coffee breaks or long lunches. They were happy to be working again and wanted to do well so that they'd be called back." The Sun Company has placed annuitants at all levels, from half-day executives to engineers and scientists assigned to special projects, to production and clerical workers. Custer's biggest concern now is to create a data bank of retiree skills so that these annuitants can fill other temporary jobs as they arise in the future.

A wide range of companies have done exactly what Sun Company envisions: drawing upon their own pool of annuitants to fill temporary positions. This option of "recalling annuitants" provides a form of postretirement employment. Northrop, with 35,000 employees at 15 domestic locations, has a standardized procedure for rehiring retirees for special assignments when particular skills are required. A Northrop retiree has the option of becoming part of the "On-Call Workforce." Members of this group may be assigned to a project that runs for several weeks to several months.

Postretirees also may be hired through secondary organizations so that postretirement employment does not affect the annuitant's pension plan with the company. Dun & Bradstreet, for instance, selects employees for this program after preretirement interviews, but actual employment contracts are arranged by an outside agency, New Life Institute. These rehirees often are used as messengers, mail clerks, and telephone operators to replace vacationing employees. The company has found that these annuitants are more reliable and require less supervision than other temporary help hired in the past.

Redesigned Jobs

In some companies, jobs have been redesigned to reduce physical burdens, stress, responsibility, or other factors that may dampen older workers' motivation to continue working. One company using the concept of job redesign is Evans Products, a national conglomerate with 16,000 employees in 400 locations that manufactures railroad cars and custom homes and maintains lumbering operations. Hiring policies at Evans are designed to accommodate older workers. The company finds older workers its most stable and reliable resource. Instances of "customized" job redesign are common throughout the organization. At the payroll department in the Evans plant in Corvallis, Oregon, the firm's payroll officer decided not to retire at 65 but asked that the company redesign her job for less responsibility. Management agreed, and she was assigned to handle the payroll for nonexempt workers only. She continued to work in this new capacity past 70, and the company was pleased enough with the arrangement to offer similar options to other older workers.

Transfer or Reassignment

A survey of 1285 managers in 154 of Denmark's largest companies found that older managers were less averse to the concept of voluntary demotion or downplacement than younger executives. Though only 8 percent of executives under age 40 surveyed would agree to being replaced by a younger employee, even if salary and title remained unchanged, nearly 75 percent of managers over 54 would accept this job change. Moreover, when this question was rephrased to include downgrading in title and responsibility, as well as a 10 percent reduction in salary, 28 percent of the 55-and-over age group said they would prefer this demotion to early retirement. Another 28 percent said they also would accept this downplacement if it entailed reduced work effort.

A few corporations in the United States have experimented with downplacement. The Maremont Company, which employes 7500 and has annual sales of $375 million, has offered older employees downplacement as an alternative to termination. The downplacement process has worked well where the affected employee was given a choice, could relocate, and received counseling during the transitional period.

Downplacement is also a successful, though unusual, policy at the Kellogg Company in Battle Creek, Michigan, where Kellogg is a major employer. Older workers who wish to assume lesser responsibilities are aided by two company policies: the advertisement of internal vacancies and the preference given to internal transfers over outside hiring. Voluntary demotion, in sum, is a policy that can benefit both the employee and company by retraining and utilizing the experience of long-time employees.

Because of their increasingly large percentage of older workers, Japanese corporations also have begun to implement new measures for accommodating aging employees. In order to prevent the aging workforce from limiting promotional opportunities for younger workers, many Japanese firms require the resignation of managers at age 55. Rather than treating mandatory retirement as an end to an employee's working life, however, these companies retain the senior executive either as a "technical specialist" or in a nonsupervisory capacity. Such a union contract recently was ratified by the five largest steel companies in Japan, and manufacturing companies such as Nissan Motor and Toshiba Electronics also have incorporated contract clauses of this type. A look at the policies of another Japanese company in the electrical appliance industry demonstrates how job reassignments can prolong the employment of senior workers. For example, this company is gradually transferring computer work from younger males to older ones. Older employees also are taking over operation of business machines at each factory. Most of the older workers reassigned to these jobs had no prior experience in these areas but were eager to acquire new skills and demonstrated satisfactory performance.

Other Japanese companies have used the concept of reassignment to transfer workers to positions that take advantage of older employees' contacts in and knowledge of particular regions. One airline company is experimenting with a "sales coordinator" position, a managerial position involving the active development of a sales network within a city. The job description for this position clearly specifies that applicants "who are near retirement and well known in their region are given preference."

In Japan, older workers also are assigned to specialized units that serve as affiliates of a company's manufacturing division. These units handle a variety of services, including maintenance and repair, technical guidance, quality inspections, administrative service, and other positions that maximize the older worker's experience and skills.

An American air freight carrier found that older workers could adjust to new jobs and maintain productivity at the same pace as younger cohorts when, after installing a highly automated and computerized container system in a traditional freight warehouse, the company allowed an initial learning period for retraining its entire workforce. About half the workforce was over 40, and, although this transfer of older workers was mandated by technological change rather than by "humanistic" design, it reflected favorably on the learning capacities of older employees.

New Careers

New career options depend on the use of intermediary organizations and personal initiative, but companies can assist a retiring employee in finding satisfying work elsewhere by offering access to secondary placement agencies, counseling, educational services, and other training and support services. Many older workers may elect to begin a business and become self-employed in their later years. A few companies on the West Coast, such as Lockheed, have engaged a specialized firm, New Career Opportunities, to teach retirees how to start small businesses.

Companies also may provide "outplacement," giving laid-off workers or mandatory retirees access to outside personnel counseling services. These services reduce both the anxiety of finding a new job and the amount of time required to do so. They also can decrease the feelings of antagonism that the ex-employee may harbor against the company. Both the number of intermediary organizations targeted for older workers and the companies' use of these services are growing. Some large companies provide their own in-house placement services.

In addition to the standard placement firms, a large number of organizations are oriented specifically to aiding retirees returning to the workforce. Mature Temps, a nationwide employment agency that provides older-worker services to its clients' companies, is one such organization. Senior Personnel Employment Council of Westchester County, New York, is a nonprofit employment service whose volunteer job counselors are senior citizens themselves.

Comprehensive and in-depth placement and counseling services provided by these secondary organizations are a vital part of the employment process for many retirees and senior citizens. They also are most helpful in facilitating corporate hiring of older workers and in encouraging older workers to return to the workplace.

Volunteerism

Given the fact that financial consideration plays a relatively minor role in retirement decisions, volunteerism is a realistic alternative. If society is unable to provide paid jobs for senior citizens, volunteer work can address the psychological imperative for meaningful activity.

A 1981 Harris survey indicated that about 23 percent of all adult Americans (37 million) engage in some form of volunteer activity. More than 4 million of these volunteers are over 65. The survey, however, gives no indication of the extent of the volunteer commitment. The absence of data on volunteerism makes it difficult to discuss the extent of opportunity for older persons; however, we do know that, compared with the general population, a smaller proportion of people over 65 engage in volunteer work. After reviewing the activities of retired Americans in 1979, the National Center of Voluntary Action concluded that very little of the retired population is channeled into community activities.

When older people do contribute their time, there is strong evidence that both the volunteers and the recipients of their services are satisfied. A study by the Academy for Educational Development indicated that 85 percent of volunteer institutions utilizing retirees rate their work as excellent or very good. The continuous expansion of public and private volunteer activities for senior citizens further attests to community receptiveness to these programs. Still, there is ample room for increased participation. Congressman Claude Pepper, Chairman of the Select Committee on Aging, stated, "The challenge of the 1980s lies in recognizing the experience, skill, and wisdom elders have to offer and in developing mechanisms that capitalize on this tremendous resource."

Empirical research confirms Pepper's view. The effects of volunteering were measured by comparing representative samples of 272 active volunteers (mean age 70) to 130 people (mean age 68) on the waiting list to become volunteers for the Senior Companion Program. The conclusions drawn from these comparisons were straightforward and positive:

1. *Volunteers are less lonely.* In response to the question, "How often do you feel lonely?" only 8 percent of the active volunteers said "quite often," as opposed to 22 percent of those waiting to be volunteers. Nearly 65 percent of the active volunteers said "almost never," versus 46 percent of those on the waiting list.

2. *Volunteers believe their help is vital.* When asked what would happen to those they serve if the program were suspended, 30 percent of the active Senior Companion volunteers thought their clients would be lonely. Another 22 percent thought their people would experience "a general negative response." Another 13 percent of these volunteers responded that their clients would not have the necessary help.

3. *The benefits of volunteering exceed expectations.* Compared with active volunteers, people waiting to be volunteers had a different pattern of responses to the question, "What would be/is the major effect of being a volunteer on your life?" Twenty-three percent of the active volunteers experienced "personal growth," while only nine

percent of the waiting-list volunteers predicted it. Only 9 percent of active volunteers said they would discontinue their involvement in the program if the stipend were removed, compared to 22 percent of those on the waiting list.

The greatest challenge is to motivate older citizens to take the first step. Providing a stipend to volunteers is one such incentive, but most financially limited organizations cannot provide remuneration. Government sponsored agencies are experiencing sharp cutbacks. Nonetheless, there are various ways that organizations can recruit and encourage volunteerism among retirees.

Companies and corporations, for instance, can play a formative role. Just as they can extend the working life of employees by providing alternative job arrangements, companies also can encourage volunteerism among their employees by initiating their own volunteer programs, specifically tailored to the needs and interests of pre- and postretirees. Timing the recruitment process for volunteers must begin during the paid work life, perhaps through expanded released time or loaned-personnel programs. Some companies also have developed their own volunteer services, staffed by both present employees and retirees.

The same kinds of management skills that seem to make workers want to remain in the workforce also are needed in the volunteer sector. There exist several major strategies that any volunteer organization should employ:

1. *Treat the older volunteer professionally and personally.* Such factors as a challenging job, interesting work, and recognition for good work are as important in the volunteer sector as they are in the private sector. One of the largest and most successful national volunteer programs, Retired Senior Volunteers Program (RSVP), has moved rapidly from a local to a national program because of its carefully organized structure and treatment of older people. All volunteers are interviewed personally by RSVP staff members before they are placed in volunteer assignments. This careful placement process insures that both the volunteer and the organization obtain maximum benefit from the volunteer's skills. In addition, RSVP staffers continuously follow up on their placements to see that the arrangement is working well for both parties. This earnest and diligent

approach is quite fitting for mature volunteers, especially if they are making the transition from corporate or professional careers to volunteer work.

Organizations that engage older people should concern themselves with the psychological and, if necessary, financial needs of the volunteer.

2. *Marshal the skills, interests, and experience of senior volunteers.* The desire for a great deal of responsibility and freedom to decide how to do one's work are as important in the voluntary sector as in the employment sector. The International Executive Service Corps of Retired Executives (SCORE) permits retired executives to use their work experience in a consultant-type arrangement, offering technical and financial advice to companies both in the United States and abroad. The Senior Companion Program and Foster Grandparents are particularly gratifying for volunteers with "people-helping" needs. Teaching–Learning Communities (T–LC) was begun in Ann Arbor, Michigan. Older volunteers who participate in T–LC may select and offer to teach whatever is of greatest importance or interest to them. Continued growth and identity reinforcement are provided for the older person, along with enthusiasm, support, and enrichment for the child. The T–LC program also uses an interview process in assessing the special interests of the volunteer.

3. *Provide flexibility and diversity in volunteer options.* Concepts of flexible work arrangements can apply to volunteer programs as well as paid employment. The greater the array of options, the better the likelihood of encouraging participation of more older people. They can provide counseling on energy conservation, taxes, insurance, medical care, personal budgeting, transportation, home repairs, legal services, community social services, hospitals, nursing homes, and school systems. They can provide information and referral activities, advocacy for local community improvements, help in using libraries, and support for recreational activities.

Volunteering also can provide marketable skills that facilitate the transition to paid work. In fact, a significant number of older people surveyed expressed a desire to use volunteer work as a stepping-stone to a new career. Thus, volunteering can provide needy older people with the same boost it gives younger people—the acquisition of experience, expertise, and acquaintance in fields of their choice.

4. *Educate the public on the phenomenon of volunteerism.* In a broad psychological sense, altruistic motivation is alien to the precepts of a market economy. Volunteers do not "compute" in the market mentality, and the very fact of their unpaid status undermines their perceived competence and value in the public mind. If volunteers in general are perceived as incompetent amateurs, the image of *senior* volunteers suffers this injustice exponentially. The myths and stereotypes affect the volunteers themselves as deeply as the general public.

5. *Apply motivational concepts to volunteer programs.* Volunteer programs are plagued by a high turnover rate. There is considerable anecdotal evidence to suggest that many of the motivational principles discussed in the preceding sections apply to paid as well as unpaid workers. On the other hand, volunteer programs constitute unique environments that require special understanding. Whereas "work itself" is the chief motivator for most paid workers, volunteers may be far more receptive to "status rewards" than paid workers. Since status symbols are always socially defined, older volunteers, when in a position of public esteem, can be highly motivated, even if the job involves objectively menial tasks. But if older workers are not valued or esteemed, their job satisfaction and motivation will wither, no matter how interesting or responsible the actual work.

In many volunteer situations, supervisors and leaders are not sufficiently demanding of their volunteers. The former may feel constrained by the lack of an economic "hold" over their unpaid workers and may even feel guilty about pushing too hard or administering the slightest semblance of discipline. Others may be undemanding simply because they have accepted the unfair volunteer stereotype and underestimate the abilities of their subordinates. By contrast, one particularly successful volunteer organization routinely fires unpaid workers who do not measure up to standard!

Volunteerism does not imply amateurism. A program dependent on volunteer staff and thus lacking the motivation of a paycheck must be designed to provide powerful incentives for personalized employment satisfaction. For paid or unpaid employees, these satisfactions derive from the following factors:

1. *A sense of competence, self-confidence, and professional development.* From the time of initial contact, volunteers should be regarded as professionals. They must be screened carefully before acceptance into the program, thoroughly trained to assume their assigned tasks, and presented with a detailed job description. When the organization shows respect for a volunteer's ability by requiring quality work and offering responsibility on a level equal to that of a salaried person, it gets reliable and professional performance in return.

2. *A feeling of accomplishment that derives from direct responsibility and knowing "how it came out."* Volunteers must be given an honest evaluation of the success or failure of their work.

3. *A sense of fulfillment, gratification, and personal growth that comes with the learning of another discipline.* There is exhilaration in using existing skills and acquiring new ones, especially learning to understand, relate to, and deal successfully with people of different cultures and lifestyles.

4. *A congenial atmosphere that provides companionship and mutual respect and the pride of being able to make a contribution, through a group, that is more significant than one can make as an individual.* Volunteers must be incorporated into the staff, not as appendages but as full participants, with the confidence that their roles are sufficiently important to be fundamental to the overall goals of a program.

CONCLUSION

All industrialized countries now find themselves in a period of unprecedented economic vulnerability. The need to provide jobs for people over 65 is only one of several competing imperatives. Equally pressing is the need to find jobs for those presently unemployed and to provide opportunities for new workers now entering the labor force. The employment problem is compounded further by advancing technologies that are eliminating jobs and occupations and creating new layers of structural unemployment. There are 32 million unemployed workers in the European Economic Community countries. Unemployment stands at the highest levels since the depression of the 1930s in all countries except Japan. A few decades ago there were four or five major competitors in the world economy; today there are more than 20 significant trading countries. Developing economies with large youthful populations, such as Korea, Singapore, and Malaysia, have become industrialized.

The needs of the elderly must be viewed against this backdrop. The competition is stern, but the goal of keeping older people productive is imperative to our individual, social, and economic survival.

REFERENCES AND BIBLIOGRAPHY

Allen, K. K., et al. (1979). *Volunteers from the workplace*. Washington, D.C.: National Center for Voluntary Action.

American Council of Life Insurance. (1982). *Older americans*. Datatrack Series. Washington, D.C.

American Institute for Research. (1977). *Jobs for older workers in U.S. industry: Possibilities and prospects*. Final Report. Washington, D.C.: Center for Work and Aging.

Americans helping each other. (1982, March). *Saturday Evening Post*, p. 90.

Anderson, K., et al. (1981, October 19). Visions of voluntarism. *Time*, pp. 47–48.

Blank, R. C. (1982). A changing worklife and retirement pattern: An historical perspective. In M. Morrison (Ed.), *Economics of aging*. New York: Van Nostrand Reinhold.

Cheatham, M. (1982, November). Voluntarism '82. *Vital speeches, 49*,40–42.

Clark, M. Unleashing the productive value of long life. In N. McCloskey & F. Borgatta (Eds.), *Aging and retirement*. Beverly Hills, Calif.: Sage.

Clark, R. L., & Menefee, J. A. (1981). Federal expenditures for the elderly: Past and future. *The Gerontologist, 21*(2).

Damm, M., et al. (1981). The older job seeker: Barriers and supports to re-employment. Paper presented at 33rd Annual Scientific Meeting, Gerontological Society of America.

Dennis, H., & Sanford, M. (1981). *The availability of older workers to the labor market*. Los Angeles, Calif.: National Policy Center on Employment and Retirement, University of Southern California.

Employer attitudes: Implications of an aging workforce. New York: William M. Mercer.

Fullerton, H. N., & Flaim, P. O. (1976, November). New labor force projections to 1990. *Monthly Labor Review*.

Generations. (1981, Summer). Special issues on Elders and Volunteerism, 5(4).

Golub, J., et al. (1982). *Emergency employment options for older workers: Practice and potential, an evaluation*. Washington, D.C.: National Commission for Employment Policy.

Golub, J. *Older Americans in the workplace: An issue review report and databook (working draft)*. Jobs in 1980s and 1990s project. New York: The Public Agenda Foundation.

Goudy, W. (1981). Changing work expectations: Findings from the retirement history study. *Gerontologist, 21*(6).

Goudy, W. (1982). Antecedent factors related to changing work expectations. *Research on Aging, 4*(2).

Graney, M. J., & Cottam, D. M. (1981). Labor force nonparticipation of older people: United States, 1890–1970. *Gerontologist, 21*(2).

Harris, Louis, & Associates. (1974). The myth and reality of aging. A study for the National Council on Aging.

Harris, Louis, & Associates. (1979, February). 1979 Study of American attitudes towards pensions and retirement: A nationwide survey of retirees and business leaders.

Harris, Louis, & Associates. (1981). Aging in the eighties: America in transition. A study for the National Council on Aging.

Jacobson, B. (1980). *Young programs for older workers: Case studies in progressive behavior*. Work in America Institute Series. New York: Van Nostrand Reinhold.

The Japan Society. (1980, June). *The aging labor force: Implications for Japan and the United States*. (A Seminar Report.) Public Affairs Series 13.

Kratcoski, P. C. (1982, January). Can volunteers save the day? *USA Today,* p. 70.

Morrison, M. (1982, December 7). Presentation at the Brookdale Institute on Aging. Columbia University.

Morrison, M. Reappraising retirement and personnel policies. In M. Mc-Closky & E. Borgotta (Eds.), *Aging and retirement*. Beverly Hills, Calif.: Sage.

National Council on Aging. *Aging in America*. Report on the Northern American Regional Technical Meeting on Aging, Washington, D.C.

Olsen, L. (1982, December 7). The macroeconomic effects of delayed retirement. Paper presented at Brookdale Institute on Aging, Columbia University.

Osako, M. M. (1982). How Japanese firms cope with effects of an aging labor force on industrial productivity. *Aging and Work*.

Parnes, H. S. (1981, December). From the middle to the later years: Longitudinal studies of the pre- and postretirement experiences of men. *Research on Aging, 3*(4).

Peterson, D. *The older worker: Myths and realities*. Los Angeles, Calif.: University of Southern California, Andrus Gerontological Center (unpublished).

The potential for growth. (1982, October). *USA Today,* p. 8.

Public Agenda Foundation. (1982). *Jobs in the 1980s and 1990s*.

Reese, M. (1981, October 5). Let volunteers do it. *Newsweek,* p. 26.

Retirement Advisers Inc. Selected older workers: policies and issues. Mimeographed handout for use at RAI Workshops.

Retiring to work. (1980, November/December). *Aging, 313 & 314*,4–12.

Root, N. (1981, March). Injuries at work are fewer among older employees. *Monthly Labor Review*.

Segerberg, D. (1982). *Living to be a hundred*. New York: Scribners.

Sheppard, H., & Mantovani, R. (1982). *Part-time employment*. Washington, D.C.: National Council on Aging.

Sheppard, H., & Rix, S. (1977). *The graying of working America*. New York: Free Press.

Stotler, M., & Stotler, E. (1981). Labor force participation among the elderly. Paper presented at 34th Annual Scientific Meeting, Gerontological Society of America.

Streib, G., & Schneider, C. (1971). *Retirement in American society*. Ithaca, N.Y.: Cornell University Press.

Tice, C. H. (1982, September/October). A gift from the older generation: Continuity. *Children Today, 11*, 2–6.

U.S. Congress, Select Committee on Aging. (1981, August). *Abolishing mandatory retirement*. 97th Congress Committee Publications #97–283. Washington, D.C.: U.S. Government Printing Office.

U.S. Department of Health, Education and Welfare. *Working with older people: A guide to practice (Vol. 1.)*. Washington, D.C.: U.S. Government Printing Office.

U.S. Department of Health, Education and Welfare. (1981). *Employment and training: Report of the president*. Washington, D.C.: U.S. Government Printing Office.

U.S. Department of Labor. (1965). *The older American workers: Age discrimination in employment*. Washington, D.C.: U.S. Government Printing Office.

Why people delay retiring. (1982, December). *Modern Maturity*.

Work in America Institute. (1980). *The future of older workers in America: New options for an extended working life*. A Work in America Policy Study. New York.

Yarmon, P. (1981, January). Sign right here to volunteer. *Fifty Plus, 21*,28–29.

6

Opportunities: A Dialogue between Betty Friedan and Maurice Lazarus

FRIEDAN:

We are going to propound certain general principles that should shape policy in our societies. We will then give hints as to how they might be applied to employment, education, housing, and health.

In general: All policies and programs affecting people over 65 should aim to maximize the highest human potential of each individual, acknowledging the lifelong physiological changes with age in terms of their reality rather than stereotype, affirming the emergence of certain unique qualities of age such as wisdom, generativity, and integration that can enhance social productivity.

In particular:

- People over 65 should be treated as part of society and not segregated as a separate class.
- Individual differences actually increase with age; they should be respected, not resented as idiosyncratic departures from the norm.
- People over 65 should have the widest possible choice of options for productive participation in society.
- People over 65 are entitled to equal rights and opportunities in society and can be expected to perform with equal responsibility.
- Political, legal, and other forms of public action are required to

    break through existing age stereotypes and to restructure insti-
    tutions so they can meet these goals.

• Age no longer should be viewed as an illness, a passive, depen-
    dent infirmity whose care and treatment is a burden on society.

• Societal and individual attitudes must be changed to release the
    human potential of the *new* years of life—the gift of the evolu-
    tion of our society—the 25 to 45 new years of life people have
    gained in this century.

LAZARUS:

In trying to address these principles, we have to come to grips with
the word "retire." When people complete four years of college, we
don't say they are retiring from college; we say they are commencing.
When they complete their graduate studies we don't say they are
retiring from the university; they are graduating. This concept of
retiring at a particular age is an anathema to the concept of productive aging. So, one of our first assignments is to find a word that
doesn't mean withdraw but that means continuing participation. It
can even mean commencement.

There are two aspects to retirement as it is now understood. One
aspect is *economic*. Pensions are savings that at a certain age are paid
back to individuals for the rest of their lives at a certain rate, based
upon the number of years they have been with an organization and
the positions they have held. They are rewards for past service.

The other aspect is *job tenure*. In most companies, after some
years of service individuals retain a particular position until retirement. There are exceptions to this rule. In Japan many company
managers can hold jobs only until age 55, but they don't then withdraw from the company; their jobs are restructured. We see the same
practice in our universities: Deans don't retire; they go back to teaching and research. Such structures encourage workers to continue to
be productive in the organization. Such encouragement could be, and
in many companies is, offered even after people reach retirement
age. They receive their pensions but are offered jobs that meet their
personal needs.

Surveys indicate that most people would like to continue to work
after age 65. Most would like to work in some restructured job. They

would like to work different hours, shorter work weeks, part time, or in shared jobs. Surveys also show that most people want to continue their involvement in the organization for which they have worked, more for psychological than economic rewards. From the company's point of view, their continued presence after age 65 can provide experience and stability not present among any other group of workers.

More and more of our working population is involved in service industries. These industries require part-time workers on a variety of schedules and readily can accommodate people who have retired but want to adjust their working schedules. Many companies with a heavy clerical component have already introduced flex-time, which permits workers to adjust their hours to permit an even broader choice of working schedules. Some industries that require particular skills have made arrangements for people to continue to work effectively at home.

After retirement, many people want to embark upon new careers and become productive in new ways. Some companies provide counseling services and educational opportunities in the later years of employment prior to retirement.

I'd just like to call attention to a pertinent event: In order to meet the problems of structural unemployment in Germany, a bill was introduced in the Bundestag to lower the retirement age to 58 instead of reducing the work week for all workers. The bill sought to solve structural unemployment in Germany on the backs of the elderly. The bill did not pass.

FRIEDAN:

Structural unemployment cannot be solved in terms of special treatment for the elderly. Given all people's needs for meaningful participation in the work of society, we now have to expand the concept of work. Rather than trying to solve the problem of unemployment on the backs of any one group—the young, the old, or women—let's introduce a six-hour work day for everyone, provide flexible options of reducing the work day or work week for everyone, and give more options for sabbaticals and education-and-work combinations throughout life.

Robert Butler once told me that he believed in retiring all your life. Instead of retirement at the upper end, deal into your life all along certain periods of refreshment, where you get out of your regular routine and open yourself to new purposes.

✓Paradoxically, with all we're learning about the human potential of the new years of age, the increase in health and vitality, and the ability to participate that Svanborg's studies in Sweden show, nations continue to lower the retirement age.

There is a concept that we developed in dealing with questions of race and sex discrimination in the United States called "affirmative action." It is not just illegal to fire or not to hire a person because she or he is black or female; it is incumbent upon the company or the institution to take affirmative action to change certain things structured into the job that keep women or black people from being hired, from being used to the best of their abilities.

Affirmative action, in terms of people over 65, would mean that a company not only would have to question its retirement policy or age standards for hiring but would have to consider restructuring the job itself. According to our evidence, older people do not like machine-paced jobs. In fact, it was the industrial revolution that gave us the concepts of retirement and unproductive aging. In rural societies, people are productive until they die. Now, machine-paced jobs are going to be less and less important in advanced industrial society; however, just as we learned to wear glasses for eye deficits, we can restructure job components to permit the continued use of human abilities with age deficits.

✓ Employing people over 65 requires reconceptualizing and finding ways of financing, rewarding, or validating work that is socially productive and traditionally has been done by volunteers. Older people might not have to be paid in cash as the means of verifying their work; they could receive health benefits, increased Social Security benefits, or tax credits. Volunteerism is important to individuals and to society; age may force society to come to new terms with it. The women's movement went through a whole phase of saying volunteer work is just a way of exploiting women and not paying them. Only after we demanded equal pay and equal opportunities for women in employment could we see that volunteer work is important and that women and men now can do it on equal terms. Age requires volunteer work that has a new basis in reality and public benefit.

LAZARUS:

Something peculiar has happened to the word "volunteer." In both world wars, we had volunteers who were air-raid wardens, nurses, and ambulance drivers; they were very important people to our society. There are volunteer magistrates in England today, and that's a dignified job. There are more things that society wants done than we can possibly get done, but we haven't found a way of dignifying the jobs that need to be done in a way that will attract volunteers. We don't have trouble doing it in emergencies; we ought to be able to do it normally.

FRIEDAN:

Education is just as important to maximizing health, productivity, and the quality of life for people over 65 as regular physical exams or medical treatment. "Use it or lose it" is true, above all, for cognitive abilities. My own research indicates, quite simply, that if you continue to use your highest human abilities you insure vital aging. Some of the principles that apply to education are:

1. *There should be no age barriers to education.* Up to now high-school, college, university, and professional-school admission has been age related. That began to change, in the United States at least, after World War II, when many older students came back from the war and got high-school and college educations. Above all, it changed when women began to return for education in their middle years. People over 65 do well and learn well and use this kind of training. Given possible life expectancies of 80 to 90 years, who knows what creative productivity will result? There is no reason at all not to admit people to any form of education without the usual age barriers, if they can meet the requirements, either formally or in terms of equivalency tests.

2. *We need to develop special, participatory forms of education that engage wisdom and other positive qualities of age.* Rather than the denigrating and patronizing pap that often characterizes special education programs for the elderly, programs should respect individual personhood. They should not treat the aged as children but in-

stead use their abilities in flexible ways with new kinds of classes where older people can be both learners and teachers at the same time. These forms of education, developed in cooperation with people over 65, also might be valuable elsewhere in educational systems. Confronting the new needs of people over 65 brings us to the cutting edge in many areas, but especially in education, which is trying to respond to the needs of our whole changing society.

3. *Professionals should be re-educated to break through their denial and stereotyping of age and see the potentials of vital, productive aging.* As we now require sex education in schools, as we require children to take shop, cooking, sewing, math, and computers, we should require our schools to provide age education or lifespan education that opens the curtain of middle age and reveals the potential of an 80-to-90-year lifespan.

In countries where all education is public, there is no special problem of financing education for the elderly. In the United States, where the student often pays for higher education, education stamps might be as important for people over 65 as food stamps.

LAZARUS:

I don't know what's happening in other countries, but it is perfectly amazing how the demand for education by working and older people is growing. Harvard University has as many students enrolled in part-time programs for credit as it has on a full-time basis, including undergraduate and graduate students. In 1983, an advanced degree in literature was given to a man of 89 years.

FRIEDAN:

As far as health is concerned, it must be the *duty* of caregivers—physicians, nurses, social workers, and nursing home personnel—to maximize the potential of the person over 65 for active human functioning. It should be considered a violation of health standards, the equivalent of malpractice, to induce dependency of the aged through overmedication or underactivity. The standard by which a health facility, nursing home, geriatrician, or general practitioner should be judged is optimum functioning. The sedations, the tranquilizations, and the bureaucratic routines that keep the aged meek and orderly— even if keeping them that way promotes cleanliness—should be considered violations of health standards, even to the point of withdrawing licenses.

A Harvard psychologist named Ellen Langer studied the nursing home situation. She took one ward and said to everybody in that ward, "You are here in the Jones Nursing Home and our job is to keep you happy. The nurse will bring each of you a plant and will water it every day so you can enjoy its beauty." The other ward was told, "You are here in the Jones Nursing Home and it is up to you if your stay here will be good for you. You have certain things in your room; you can rearrange them as you like. The nurse will bring each of you a plant and tell you what needs to be done to take care of the plant and it is up to you to water the plant." Within the next few months the patients who were given the responsibility of watering the plants showed the greatest improvement on all sorts of indices of health and well-being, when compared to the others. Two years later, when Langer went back for a follow-up study, the patients who watered the plants were alive; most of those patients who were just taken care of were dead.

The evidence shows that even supposed handicaps and deteriorations can be reversed by tasks, by exercise, by responsibilities, by environmental changes. They should not be viewed as "exceptional" phenomena; in terms of the principles we have put forward, they define good health care for the elderly.

LAZARUS:

The real job of the physician is to keep the elderly independently functional. According to Svanborg's figures (see Chapter 7 of this book, p. 90), 95 percent of the 70 year olds, 90 percent of the 75 year olds, and 80 percent of the 79 year olds are without advanced handicap. To help them stay that way shouldn't be an onerous assignment for physicians. The other task, which James Birren emphasized very dramatically, is promoting health practices that will intensify and prolong the functionality of these age groups.

FRIEDAN:

As to housing, we all agree that it is better for older people to live with their own families than in nursing homes or other institutions. Yet, realistically, even the developing nations say that the family as it has been previously defined is not going to be the answer in the future for a great many people. So family bonds must and can be reinterpreted. This will require new forms of physical housing for "families of choice," arrangements in which people of different age and sex come to dwell together without genetic or legal ties.

LAZARUS:

We must offer the widest choice of housing options that society can afford. There is no one answer. Many elderly want to live with their peers, but those who feel the need to replicate their family situation may feel happier and more productive living in mixed-age housing situations. They have been tried successfully in Scandinavia, where the elderly have the benefits of living in a younger community and are able to assume responsibilities for babysitting and the like while younger parents work. Neighbors are helping neighbors, but it's intergenerational. It seems to me that trying to find *the* answer to housing the elderly is probably a great mistake. We have to provide as many options as we possibly can and as many techniques in terms of experimenting with new ways in which the elderly and the young, where that is appropriate, can participate in innovative housing arrangements.

FRIEDAN:

To bring about this new concept of the years over 65 as promising and productive rather than childish, sick, passive, alone, and senile, we must have a campaign against stereotypes and for reality in the media. In the United States today it is not acceptable in an advertising commerical to show black people as shiftless and less than fully human, or women as dumb and helpless. It is quite possible to change other stereotypes in the mass media and in the textbooks. We must show people over 65 as participants in all kinds of activities in which they are actually engaged. They need to be shown as participants, with the special qualities of wisdom that James Birren talks about. Furthering knowledge about the defenses and denials of our own aging also may combat our reluctance to deal with problems of age in ourselves as individuals and as policy makers in industry and government. Education about denial and defense with some media elucidation would enhance vital aging.

A political movement will be required to liberate the potential of vital aging in all of our nations. I'm using the word political in the largest sense. We have to break through stereotypes of ageism, just as in many societies we had to break through stereotypes of racism and sexism. We have to break through the legal and habitual barriers that keep older people from employment and educational opportunities.

In advanced nations during the last decades of this century, the movement of people in their sixties, seventies, and eighties—the movement of older people toward full personhood, full participation in the society—will be as world shaking as the women's movement or the movement of the oppressed races. We must beware of the experts, the professional and institutional establishments who keep elders quiet and passive. To liberate the vital potential of the new years of life, the people who are themselves in these years will have to demand the things that they need. In doing so they will break through the stereotypes.

Policies and programs of, by, and for the aged alone, apart from society as a whole, are not enough here. Unions and progressive political movements will have to address themselves actively to questions of restructuring employment and education all along the line. The political movement need not pit the aged against the rest of society. New alliances are needed that use the new demographic political strength of the aging group in the restructuring of work in ways that meet not only the needs of older workers but also the needs of people in the child-rearing years and people of any age who want to combine work and education. This movement will use the integrative wisdom of the aged to form new kinds of coalitions on human needs that cross the age, sex, and class polarizations of the past.

7

Health, Productivity, and Aging: Interventions

Alvar Svanborg

At Salzburg we set out to change incorrect negative attitudes toward the ability of the elderly. We began by asking, "To what extent are the elderly able to contribute in a meaningful way to the productivity of our societies?"

Old and tired! Old and weak! Old and sick! As an advisor to organizations and governments I have been asked several times to provide medical reasons for a further lowering of the retirement age. Many of the Fellows at Salzburg had been confronted with the same request, particularly in societies with high rates of unemployment and automation.

Some people seem to believe that the best way to minimize negative attitudes is to push the pendulum over to an unrealistically positive attitude. I think, however, that only well-grounded facts accumulated through different forms of gerontological research will be persuasive.

There seem to be at least three negative attitudes standing in the way of using the reserve of productivity that the elderly possess. The first arises from the belief that, since our cells and organs have only a limited storage of energy-producing capacity left at old age, low usage of these resources will prolong life. Recent research indicates the opposite, namely, that cells, organs, and the whole individual need the stimulation of being used. Conversely, inactivity generally is more negative and dangerous than activity. To give just one example: Thrombosis, which causes disturbed circulation, is a common disorder in the elderly, but the incidence becomes much higher during periods of inactivity.

The second negative attitude toward the productive ability of the elderly arises from the belief that all elderly are impaired, both by aging and illness. In fact, at the age of 70 at least 30 to 40 percent are lacking any symptoms of definable disorders. Among the 60 to 70 percent with such symptoms, the majority suffer from disorders that do not make them incapable of productive and meaningful contribution in our society. Many younger people who still are working actively have the same symptoms as those elderly, such as cutaneous diseases, back pain, and affective mental disorders. We know that activity within wide limits often has therapeutic and prophylactic effect. Use of the productive ability of the elderly not only would tap wasted resource but also would prevent and postpone disability.

Many of the observations mentioned in Chapter 2 illustrate the great interindividual variations, especially in the age interval 65 to 75. These findings warn against segregation of the elderly as a group. Still, it is necessary to accept certain forms of statistical grouping for societal planning. There is a more rapid increase in impairment, disability, and handicap in Scandinavia between the ages of 75 and 79. In planning both care and improved productivity for the elderly, a grouping into a special age interval such as "79 and over" seems to be realistic. We should be aware, however, that there are at ages above 79 many vital and productive "old-olds" who have, in comparison with all other age groups, a unique experience, namely, what life is like at 80 and above. We also need that knowledge when we want to broaden our perspective to cover a wider lifespan.

The third negative attitude toward productivity of the elderly is the set of dichotomies of good and bad, beautiful and ugly, productive and nonproductive that we formed when we were young, strong, and sometimes beautiful. An old face can have beauty never present in the young. An old person need not be old-fashioned in an unproductive way but may possess a range of experiences often called wisdom.

In clinical medicine we also have compared the elderly with the young, instead of comparing healthy olds with sick olds. I am sure that in the future, when we know more about "normality" in the elderly, we will be able not only to avoid under- and overdiagnosis, but to improve our possibilities for a more correct and individualized analysis of the performance ability of the elderly. The coming generations of physicians will be expected not only to know the occurrence of medically definable disorders but, in a broader sense, to make an assessment of both abilities and needs of elderly individuals.

Within medicine today we can measure people's functional performance instead of classifying them according to chronological age. Our studies show, for example, that neither gray hair nor wrinkles around the eyes nor psychomotoric speed are reliable indicators of the degree of age-related decline in renal function, for example. It seems reasonable to anticipate that within a few years methods for an individualized functional analysis will be available and will be encouraged for economic reasons.

In order to change the negative attitudes toward productivity of the elderly we need not only longitudinal studies that illustrate the capacity for health and productivity of the elderly, but we also need systematic intervention studies to convince ourselves, the elderly themselves, and policy makers that our stereotypes are erroneous. To illustrate these ideas in a more concrete way I shall describe the three aims of our intervention program in Gothenburg, as follows:

1. *Early and correct diagnosis and treatment.* Better quality is not greater quantity of medical service. Two examples of underdiagnosed impairments in the elderly are urinary incontinence and balance and gait disturbances. To clarify different causes of these problems and introduce possible forms of treatment and aids is of great importance for the elderly who suffer from these problems.

2. *Improved options for meaningful life and productivity.* Devices such as better lighting and eyeglasses that might improve quality of life and enhance productivity need to be identified and provided. Generally only 10 to 15 percent of the 70 year olds who declared that their only hobby was reading had adequate illumination above their reading place. Advanced visual handicap was uncommon at age 70. At maximal correction with glasses, a reduction of visual capacity to 50 to 70 percent of "normal" capacity was found in only 9 percent of 70 year olds. A reduction to 20 to 50 percent of "normal" capacity was found in 2 percent, and to 5 to 10 percent of "normal" capacity in only 1 percent. Ninety-seven percent of 70 year olds were able to read the standardized text on medicine bottles and other packages of drugs.

From many other points of view we have found that the elderly usually have much greater intellectual and physical capacities than generally thought. At age 70, 95 percent are lacking advanced handicap; at age 75, the figure is 90 percent; and at age 79, it is 80 percent.

3. *Prevention/postponing risk-factor influence*. Examples of preventive measures included in our programs are many. Accidents are common in the elderly. When we analyzed where, when, and, if possible, why hip fractures occurred, we found, contrary to what is usually believed, that only 5 percent occurred in the bathroom. The majority took place in the living room, bedroom, or kitchen. Architects should try to adjust homes in order to prevent or postpone accidents; they also should try to find out to what extent the homes of the elderly can be adapted to a better level of activity. We also need to examine the larger environment. The study of 70 year olds in Gothenburg showed that the time usually available for pedestrians at street intersections (1.4 minutes) is not adequate to allow many elderly to walk across. In Sweden, traffic accidents involving pedestrians are proportionately much more common in people aged 65 and over, even in comparison with another high-risk age group, children aged 5 to 14. Lethal outcome is about four times higher in ages 65 and above than in ages 5 through 14, and 48 percent of killed pedestrians are 65 and above (Lundegren-Lindquist, Aniansson, & Rundgren, 1983). A part of the intervention program includes altering the crosswalk time allowed by the traffic light at street intersections and reducing the step heights of pavements, buses, trains, and the like.

To what extent might it be possible to change the present trend of increasing incidence of hip fractures? Our cohort studies described in Chapter 2 have revealed direct evidence for future reduction in the density of the skeleton among the elderly. At present we know of at least four possible reasons for this. One is the negative effects of smoking and alcohol abuse. Second, many studies indicate that the intake of calcium should be higher than we found in more than 40 percent of otherwise well-nourished elderly in Gothenburg (Steen, Isaksson, & Svanborg, 1977). The third factor is a lack of regular exposure to ultraviolet light. A fourth reason may be lowered physical activity.

It usually has been thought that stimulation of the skeleton by physical loading should take place mainly at younger ages. Several recent studies show, however, that in old age physical inactivity increases the risk of osteoporosis. This implies that continuous reasonable physical loading will decrease the rate of decline of the density of the skeleton. Perhaps elderly people should have to get permission to lie down rather than get up.

In summary, our studies have shown that activity is much more feasible for elderly people than we assume, that activity is salubrious, and that we should identify and eliminate societal barriers to it.

REFERENCES AND BIBLIOGRAPHY

Lundgren-Lindquist, B., Aniansson, A., & Rundgren, Å. (1983). Functional studies in 79-year-olds. III. Walking performance and climbing capacity. *Scand. J. Rehabil. Med.*, *15*, 125.

Steen, B., Isaksson, B., & Svanborg, A. (1977). Intake of energy and nutrients and meal habits in 70-year-old males and females in Gothenburg, Sweden. A population study. *Acta Med. Scand.* (Suppl. 611), 39–86.

Svanborg, A., Bergström, G., & Mellström, D. (1982). *Epidemiological studies on social and medical conditions of the elderly. Report on a survey.* (EURO reports and studies 62.) Copenhagen, Denmark: World Health Organization.

8

Changing Sex Roles: Vital Aging

Betty Friedan

Up to now evolution has been defined in terms of reproduction of the species. The role of woman and man as traditionally defined was based primarily on reproductive differences. Even as a feminist, I have never seen any reason to deny those differences. There *are* biological differences between woman and man, differences linked to reproduction. And I don't dispute the contentions of the social biologists that polarized sex roles were conducive to survival in earlier periods of human history. In the hunting, cave-man era, men specialized in responding aggressively and women specialized in nurturing the young.

Now, however, there is a new factor: the long period of human life after reproduction. The lifespan for woman is approaching 80 years. After bearing and rearing her young, a woman still has one-third to half of her life left. Men also are living longer, though, for reasons I will discuss later, not quite so long as women. It is a new evolutionary phenomenon for this or any species to have so many years of life beyond reproduction. In this new third of life, which the Portuguese and the French call the third age, the possibilities for growth and evolution have been blurred, distorted, or denied by age stereotypes based on the experience of youth. These new possibilities even have been seen as pathologies measured only as declines from the standards set by youth. That distortion has been compounded by sex-role stereotypes, because our definitions of aging and the standards against which aging is measured have been based mainly on male experience. The blind spots caused by our excessive youth and male orientation—feminine mystique compounded by age mystique—have kept us from even confronting the startling implications of the decline of men and the flourishing of women in this third age.

As Alvar Svanborg points out in Chapter 2, there is a dramatic improvement in the life expectancy of women and an increasing divergence in life expectancy between women and men that has occurred in the last decade. This difference in life expectancy is present even in the early years, but it becomes most striking after the reproductive years. It is vastly higher in the most industrialized societies than it is in rural societies. In Jordan the life expectancy at birth is 52 years for women and 56 years for men. In Egypt, the life expectancy at birth is 53.8 for women and 51.6 for men. In Israel it is 75 for women and 71.5 for men; in Italy it is 74.9 for women and 69 for men; in France, 77.2 for women, 69.2 for men; in Sweden, 78.1 for women, 72.2 for men; in Finland, 77.1 for women, 68 for men. In the United States at the turn of the century there was only a two-year difference in life expectancy between women and men. In 1950 it was five years. Now it is eight years. Straight-line projections, which for reasons I will discuss later I think are wrong, show that by 2020 there will be a 12-year difference.

How do we explain this phenomenon? Some studies suggest that prior smoking habits make the difference. I believe more explanation lies in strengths that have been specialized in women in the interests of their reproductive role which have not been conceptualized because they came from women's private experience, primarily in the home.

In the past, women were seen as men *manqué*, or wanting by measures based solely on the experience of men. When women were denied some of the opportunities and the skills that were open to men, they were, in fact, deficient. Women needed these skills and opportunities to move in society. This change was made conscious by the women's movement, but the women's movement itself came about primarily because of these new years of human life, the third age, which women could no longer live in terms of a childbearing role alone. They had to move to a new definition of themselves in society, and they did it first in their consciousness and then in confronting social barriers and mundane conditions of daily life, moving into new roles in the work world and making active use of their abilities.

Women today have more of a sense of control over their lives, which is as important psychologically and biologically perhaps as actual control itself. Women have more sense of self-worth. Women have moved to new purposes beyond the roles of marriage and motherhood. They have moved to further education and to increased participation in society.

In the United States there have been studies that show a dramatic improvement in mental health in aging women as compared to men in the last 15 years. In the Midtown Manhattan Study (Strole, Langnor, et al., 1962), in a cohort studied in 1954 at the ages of 40 to 49, 21 percent of the women were impaired, compared to only 9 percent of the men. When studied in 1974 only 8 percent of the women in that cohort were impaired, compared to 9 percent of the men. When studied in 1954, 26 percent of the women aged 50 to 59 were impaired, compared to 15 percent of the men. When studied in 1974, only 11 percent of women in their fifties were impaired, compared to 9 percent of the men. In other words, women in the United States showed a 14-percent reduction in impairment in their forties and fifties in those 20 years, whereas men in their forties showed no reduction in impairment and in their fifties had 6 percent reduction.

There is some question as to the validity of the sample in the Midtown Manhattan follow-up study, but other studies at the National Center for Health Statistics (Granick & Patterson, 1971) confirm the striking differences between women and men and support the evidence of new patterns of aging, especially among women, that challenge the previous assumptions of declining mental health with age, increased depression with age, and increased impairment with age.

Twenty years later, in 1974, when those demographers, epidemiologists, and psychiatrists went back to the data from their original 1954 sample, they expected to see increased impairment. When their data did not show increased impairment, they were incredulous. Then, when they found that this was true only for women and not for men, they searched for clues in the changes in women's lives in this period. There has been, of course, a dramatic change in women's lives in the period from 1954 to 1974, in women's sense of themselves, their self-definition, their treatment by society, and their own behavior.

A study done by Rosalind Barnett and Grace Baruch (1984) of the

Wellesley Center for Research on Women, published in *Lifeprints,*
compared women of 35 to 55 in all sorts of combinations of roles and
found, as did the Midtown Manhattan Study, that, instead of the
expected decline of mental health or of health generally with age,
most women experienced a sense of resurgence, of revitalization, a
new sense of self and self-worth that gave them great confidence, an
openness to change, a flexibility about change, an eagerness for challenge. Those women who were studied at age 55, when asked about
age, said, "Well, I have mastered this change, and my life is so much
better now; so the next change is not a great fear for me. Why should
I be afraid of it?"

During this same period, the American Psychiatric Association
ruled out any further use of the diagnostic term *involutional melancholia. Involutional melancholia* no longer seems to occur among
women in the United States. This supposed menopausal-connected
mental disease or impairment that was so drastic is no longer filling
our mental hospitals. Women no longer suffer it, or if they do, it is
clearly pathological, not a natural product of menopause.

It was striking to me that the sense of self-worth and openness to
change and challenge was found more strongly, not among the high-
est-status, lifelong professional women, but among women who had
lived some years as housewives and then moved into work roles.
Women who had been in careers or professions all along had a strong
sense of self-worth and control over their lives, but they didn't have
this same sort of zest for change, the striking sense of a kind of ability
to master challenges and move on to new things that was evident
among women who had come from a more traditional housewife role
to new growth in midlife.

The Baruch and Barnett study (1984) showed that women who
combined marriage, motherhood, and work were in the greatest state
of psychological well-being. Of the factors necessary for psychological
well-being, the most important was a sense of control over one's life.
In that, the woman who was limited to the housewife role was deficient. She did not have as much sense of control over her life as the
woman who combined job or profession with marriage and motherhood. The second important measure, not so important for psychological well-being but still very important, was intimacy. Women who
were never married, or women who were neither married nor
mothers, were lacking in that regard. The women who combined

marriage, motherhood, and job or profession—marriage or motherhood because both or either gave that needed intimacy—were best
off in terms of well-being. Combining the two roles seemed to give
them greater control over their lives, buffering the more burdensome
part of either role.

Now I want to speculate on some traits that women bring with
them from the traditional role—which may well have a biological
basis—to their lives in advanced industrial society, traits that may be
conducive to their greater vitality, their longer life expectancy, and
greater health in age. And I want to speculate as to what aspects of
the male role, however conducive to survival in an earlier period of
evolution, might explain men's greater vulnerability at this moment
in the more industrialized societies. And then I want to speculate on
how transcending the traditional female role and integrating previous
masculine opportunities are conducive to health and vital aging in
women, and how this transcendence or integration might happen in
men.

Consider studies of coronary heart disease, which is now the
leading killer in America and in some of the other highly industrialized nations and which has been striking men in a ratio of about eight
to one, compared to women. It had been speculated that, as women
moved into traditionally male jobs and professions, they would start
suffering the so-called "Type A," hard-driven, competitive personality
syndrome that seems to be found among men more subject to coronary heart disease. Studies show that Type A men are 50 percent
more likely to suffer coronary heart disease than less competitive,
driven men. But coronary heart disease still strikes men eight times
more often than women. The incidence of coronary heart disease
increased drastically in the 1950s and 1960s in the United States. It
has since increased dramatically in other industrialized nations, while
in the United States, between 1968 and 1978, there was a decline of
21 percent in mortality from coronary heart disease. Women don't
suffer coronary heart attacks very much, but the percentage of reduction was greater among women than men. The Framingham and
other studies indicate that women in clerical service jobs with bosses
who elicited an enormous amount of hostility, with otherwise bad
bosses, with very unsupportive bosses, have about twice as much
heart disease as other women. They were women who had a lot of
suppressed hostility, no control at all in their work life, but a lot of

family responsibilities at home. These women showed an increase in coronary heart disease, much like men at a middle level who don't have control over their lives.

Let's look at women's situation. In *The Second Stage*, I described two modes of leadership and of coping with life. One mode is characterized by dominance, by either/or, zero/sum thinking, by a demand for absolute control and mastery over a situation. This win/lose, agressive, dominant, competitive mode of leadership, Type A, has been considered masculine. The other mode, Type B, is characterized by the flexibility of a both/and attitude, not either/or. The ability to live with contradictions, with complexity, and with a certain degree of ambiguity, in situations that cannot be completely dominated, is considered feminine. It is characterized by the flexibility needed in dealing primarily with people and not with things, with fluid, changing phenomena as opposed to rigid, static situations.

The description of this mode did not come from feminists; rather, it came from some business research consultants (Stanford Research Institute) who were brought in by military, business, and government institutions to deal with their own crisis in leadership and executive training. This flexible mode, Type B, these researchers said, has up to now been used only in small groups such as the family. For the woman who was in charge of the family, the domestic routine involved constant flexibility, dealing with growing children in a process of complex change that never can be controlled completely. Women have to live with complexity, live with change, and respond to these changes in continually changing ways. And, as anyone knows who has brought up children, the either/or, win/lose confrontations usually don't work; life demands a more flexible approach. Without anybody's ever defining it as such, women had to live with this kind of complexity all along in their dealings with children and men.

It may be surprising that I should point to strengths that may come from woman's traditional role, but it's not necessary to get hung up on the biological or cultural basis of these traits. Women are more sensitive to changes in the environment and more sensitive to faint signals or stimuli than men, and they seem to be this way at an early age. The social biologists would say that women with such genetic equipment would be more likely to bring up offspring who would survive and reproduce. But women's sensitivity is also enhanced by experiences with these young beings. Women learn to be more sensitive to those beings from an early age, in dealing with them as they grow up.

When women have no sense of control over their lives, they do not show that same vitality in age. When women have no purposes or goals or sense of themselves, their lives decline from childbearing down; once the children are grown, women don't have any further use for their abilities. But women who move with more self-confidence and sense of control of their lives toward new goals and presence in society can continue to use their openness, their flexibility—the strengths they have acquired in their traditional role—in ways that give them continued growth, continued vitality, continued activity, continued productivity.

Now let's look at men. Men have been specialized to the thing-dominated, thing-paced regime of advanced industrial society. But the domination that men were brought up to exert is not as functional today as it was in the cave-man era or even in the early industrial revolution. Now men are in the factory or the office, undergoing post-industrial technological change; now men's dominance over things—which led to great advances of industrial society, which put men into routinized, computerized offices, factories, professional lives, and traffic jams—has increasingly abstracted them from dealing with life itself. Farmers, like those who bring up children, can never completely control or dominate the complex process of growth, but they have in some sense more control and more flexibility built into their lives than corporate managers or assembly-line workers. The farmer's life is more geared to changing life itself.

How much control has a man who is specialized to his instrumental role in industrial society? Very few men can achieve control in the conditions of advanced industrial society. In industrial society, the men who suffer Type A stress-induced heart disease are not the few men who have dominance—the managers—but the great majority who still are driving themselves and pressuring themselves in search of it. These are men who, in fact, have little control over their lives because they work in jobs that have been routinized in industrial society. And their lives, their socialization as men, have not given them the flexibility and the sensitive attunement to human feelings that are conditions of intimacy and that seem to be part of women's strength.

According to some studies, despite the caricatures of "dress for success," most women as they move into the work world are finding a kind of satisfaction that comes not from competitive dominance but from a sense that their lives have been enlarged by combining work and home. In contrast, men in the United States are beginning to show a sense of self-doubt and a lesser commitment to "the job" that once was the absolute definition of their lives and roles.

This relaxation of roles began to manifest itself in that same period, beginning in the 1960s and going into the 1970s, when coronary heart disease among men began to decline. Studies of men in Chicago, Michigan, and elsewhere, as well as large national studies by Yankelovich, Harris, and Gallup (Friedman & Rosenman, 1974; Rosenman & Associates, 1964), indicate that at this time a value change was taking place among American men. There is in men now an increased feeling for values beyond success and dominance—values of growth, intimacy, self-realization—that came in part in response to the women's movement. But it's coming in a different way among men. There is a new yearning in men for growth, self-realization, sometimes, I believe, misinterpreted and maligned in the "me generation." This is a hint, at least, in America of a striving toward certain goals of human development, human values, and self-realization that could not be contemplated by a society that until now has been dominated by ideals of material wealth.

This change in values among men came sharply into consciousness in 1968. Then it was called the "counterculture," but now this value change has spread into the mainstream of society, as measured by Gallup and other pollsters. Even the "yuppies'" definition of "the good life"—made materially possible incidentally by the two-income family—includes some of these values. In other words, in the 1970s, while the women's movement was happening, men began to sense that there was more in life than just success or dominance according to the previous definition of the masculine role. It is my feeling that women have proceeded further in making breakthroughs in the limitations of their previously defined female role than men have of theirs. Women have broken through passivity to activity; from dependence to more control over their lives; from being defined by men as wives, mothers, and housewives to defining themselves by their own movement. As they find their own voice, I believe women will not completely follow the male model but will use some of the strengths that have come from their female experience. Men have not made such a breakthrough yet; they are in a transition state showing the need for it. It is not so easy for men, though the stake for men may be life itself.

What breakthrough for men would enable them to integrate masculine and feminine strengths in the way women are now doing, which has led to this new vitality in age for women while men now suffer midlife crises and die of premature heart attacks? In the decade following 1968, there was a 20-percent decrease in coronary heart disease. The medical experts seem to agree that much of the explanation lies in environmental changes, less cigarette smoking, and more exercise. But there is also a value change that began in the 1960s, a questioning of machismo, a loosening of the demands of that rigid masculine role, as women began to share the earning function and forced men to new questioning of their roles. We have seen, for instance, executives resisting transfers, for family reasons or community considerations; we have seen young men in business or unions demanding values other than just more money in their work.

There is a sense, even in the most powerful institutions—the military, government, or corporate bureaucracy—that different qualities of management are needed now, ones that are less macho and more geared to human sensitivities. Men, too, must be able to deal with people and to deal with change, since most of the problems in our society today do not have to do with the domination of things but with people who resist domination.

Somehow, all this becomes clearer and more urgent as we focus on age in terms of productivity and health. This integration of masculine and feminine strengths in both women and men might be what James Birren calls wisdom. It seems to involve a certain amount of flexibility, a certain amount of being able to deal with complexity and to deal with change, an ability to have some control over one's environment and yet not to have one's well-being depend on absolute control. It requires an ability to risk changes in life and then to have a sense, from having risked and mastered changes, that one can move easily to new goals and new challenges and new changes. This comes more easily to women perhaps as a result of having to deal with the discontinuities in life that their biology keeps presenting. In the decades of the women's movement, a new self-definition has occurred in early or middle adulthood. The changes women have made in their lives, the risks they have taken, demanding and learning to juggle new roles in society beyond their biological role, the strengths and flexibilities they had or acquired, have put women today in a place where age holds less fear than it does for men.

David Gutmann (1969, 1977, 1978), an eminent social scientist at Northwestern Medical School, reports on a "crossover" in midlife that he finds in many cultures—a crossover where men and women "trade" their previously held masculine or feminine roles. His theory is that women, in their early years, for the sake of parenting, have to suppress their aggressive capacities in order to concentrate on nurturing their children. In contrast, men have to exaggerate their dominance to protect the family. Then at midlife, the woman, finished with nurture, can move toward developing those aggressive traits that are part of the nature of both women and men. Men, meanwhile, move to a similar crossover and become more passive and more nurturing and expressive of feelings that they have suppressed before. He found some societies—the Druse, for instance—where this crossover is conceptualized. At the birth of the first grandchild, the cultivation of the vineyards and the fields and the shepherding of the flocks is handed over to the wife and the sons, and the man moves to a new role of commerce with the gods.

In our modern technological society, women in my generation moved from their years of nurture to new roles in society that previously had been mapped only by men. They experienced zest, rebirth, and an enormous new sense of growth and purpose. As a result, they are continuing to grow with age, in contrast to the progressive decline men experience.

What are the new roles for men? If they are going to suffer a midlife crisis, if they cannot in advanced technological society have that kind of complete dominance and complete control that used to characterize masculinity, are they going to continue to show this rate of susceptibility to coronary heart disease that is eight times higher than that of women? Or are men going to move to a new sense of what being a man is, a sense that incorporates feelings, openness to life, and other needs and satisfactions? Will they too enter a vigorous third age, just as women found a new vitality by integrating an active sense of self and mastery with their traditional sensitivities to life?

In a way, our inability to see age in terms other than senility, impairment, the crock in the nursing home—our very inability to see age as productive—comes from the fact that our definition of productivity up to now has been in the masculine terms of dominance and control, the thing-defined, thing-producing mode of industrial society of the last century. We have to break through the mystique of masculine youth in order to come to grips with the problems and the possibilities of continued productivity, of human functioning, of social vitality, even the new possibilities of human growth in these years beyond reproduction—the possibilities that this evolutionary accident have opened to us all.

The male and female strengths and roles that were specialized in the interests of reproduction can be integrated and used in new ways in these new years, to what end none of us can foresee. There will have to be new thinking, new definitions of roles in order to meet the need of society for a new kind of productivity. Women's move to productive entrance into the work of society beyond the home—public work, not just private work—converged at a time when machines were taking over routine work and the needs of society were shifting toward service industries.

The wisdom of age may be more useful to postindustrial society than thing-mastery. At Salzburg a Fellow from Poland told us about factories that had been converted to advanced technology. When this or that part of the machine went out of gear, workers who had been forced to retire at 55 were brought back because only their wisdom and experience could keep the whole thing running.

We may be entering an era in which advanced societies place increased value on human capacities, human services, human intuition, and human ability to deal with complex, flexible, changing life situations—abilities that women in some way were specialized to deal with all along. A new value will be accorded to that wisdom attained by men and women who manage to transcend and integrate previous sex role differences. Now that man's technology has enabled us to destroy our world, women's capacities become essential for human survival. To assure productive aging, we must develop the ability to transcend masculine/feminine polarization; we must integrate female strengths and male strengths into the human strengths of flexibility, intuition, and wisdom—the fruits of age.

So we must break through our stereotypes, the mystique of power, success, and productivity that has been geared to masculine values and has stopped at youth. We must break through in a way that integrates not only traits previously defined as masculine or feminine, but also the old values of youth and the new values, not yet clearly seen, of age. We have to elucidate them to get a clear picture of the true potential for health, productivity, and aging. An elucidation of such values is also needed to look at aging in its own terms, not just in terms of the values of youth, but as we have had to begin to look at female experience in its own terms in order to understand its strengths.

We are on the cutting edge of human evolution. We must see the new years of life—this third age—as a gift, a promise, a challenge, an opportunity to integrate traditional differences into new qualities which will enable the human species to survive.

REFERENCES

Baruch, G., Barnett, R., & Rivers, C. (1984). *Lifeprints: New patterns of love and work for today's woman*. New York: New American Library.

Friedman, M., & Rosenman, R. H. (1974). *Type A behavior and your heart*. New York: Knopf.

Granick, S., & Patterson, R. D. (1971). *Human aging II: An eleven year biomedical and behavioral study*. U.S. Public Health Service Monograph. Washington, D.C.: U.S. Government Printing Office.

Gutmann, D. L. (1969). The country of old men: Cross-cultural studies. *Occasional papers in gerontology, No. 5*. Ann Arbor, MI: University of Michigan.

Gutmann, D. L. (1977). Notes toward a comparative psychology of aging. In J. Birren & K. Schaie (Eds.), *The handbook of the psychology of aging*. New York: Van Nostrand.

Gutmann, D. L. (1978). Personal transformation in the post-parental period: A cross cultural view. Paper presented at the American Association for the Advancement of Science.

Rosenman, R. H., & Associates. (1964). A predicted study of coronary heart disease: The western collaborative group study. *Journal of the American Medical Association, 189* (1), 15–22.

Strole, T. S., Langnor, S. T., et al. (1962). *Mental health in the metropolis*. New York: McGraw-Hill.

9

Financing Medical and Health Care for Older Americans

Herbert P. Gleason

Medical care for older Americans is financed principally by Medicare—a federal program that reimburses people who are over 65 or disabled for the costs of certain major illnesses. Older Americans who have exhausted their Medicare benefits and have no other insurance or personal resources may be reimbursed by Medicaid—a joint state and federal program that pays a portion of medical expenses for low-income people, the amount and extent varying from state to state.

The two programs differ fundamentally in concept. *Medicare* is an entitlement program available without regard to a person's financial status. It is built on an insurance model, directed toward softening the financial impact of treating illness, particularly in hospitals. It is not directed toward keeping people healthy. *Medicaid* is an extension of the public welfare system, helping low-income people pay for medical care, along with food and housing. It may not be adequate or fair, but it is not prohibited by statute from reimbursing certain providers for specific treatments of particular maladies. Ironically, the Medicare program, which was proposed to care for virtually all older Americans, is less conducive to their health and productivity than Medicaid, which was designed to help the poor alone.

WHAT MEDICARE IS

Medicare was created by the U.S. Congress in 1965 (P.L. 89-97, 42 U.S.C. §1395). It is entitled "Health Insurance," but in fact it is "sickness insurance." Discussions of health policy in the United

States frequently are tangled up in misnomers: We usually call medical care "health care," just as we call medical insurance "health insurance." The semantic confusion often forestalls useful discussion about substance.

Medicare was designed to take care of people when they are sick, especially when they are acutely sick and require hospitalization. In addition to room and board, it will contribute to the cost of nursing, tests, drugs, physical and other therapy, and appliances provided in a hospital.

Coverage is limited to 90 days of inpatient hospital services during a single "spell of illness," subject to increasing co-payments. In addition there are 60 "reserve days" that may be spent during a lifetime. If a patient is transferred to a "skilled nursing facility" after at least three days of hospitalization, Medicare will contribute to the cost of a stay there, up to 100 days. Coverage of another inpatient stay cannot resume until the patient has been out of a hospital or nursing home for 60 days.

Medicare also contributes to the cost of physicians' services out of hospital and to very limited coverage for intermittent home health care services if the patient is homebound and under a doctor's care. The following quote is an example of a patient who would be eligible for service: "The blind diabetic who self-injects insulin may have a medically predictable recurring need for a skilled nursing visit at least every 90 days" (Home Health Agency Manual HIM-11; Commerce Clearing House Medicare and Medicaid Guide ¶1448).

Some medical social services are covered. "However, if . . . the medical social services furnished are of a type directed toward minimizing the problems any illness may create for any patient and his or her family (e.g. encouraging them to ventilate their concerns and providing them with reassurance), such services would not be considered reasonable and necessary to the treatment of the individual's illness or injury" (Commerce Clearing House Medicare and Medicaid Guide ¶1406). Also excluded from coverage to the home-bound are meals on wheels, housekeeping services, and drugs, unless they can be subsumed under Part B of Medicare, which covers certain physician's services and emergency and outpatient services in hospitals and rural health centers. Services in urban health centers are not eligible for reimbursement. Specifically excluded *by statute* from coverage are:

1. Routine physical checkups, eyeglasses or eye examinations for the purpose of prescribing, fitting, or changing eyeglasses, procedures performed (during the course of any eye examination) to determine the refractive status of the eyes, hearing aids or examinations therefor, or immunizations
2. Orthopedic shoes or other supportive devices for the feet
3. Services in connection with the care, treatment, filling, removal, or replacement of teeth or structures directly supporting teeth, except that payment may be made under part A in the case of inpatient hospital services in connection with the provision of such dental services if the individual, because of his underlying medical condition and clinical status or because of the severity of the dental procedure, requires hospitalization in connection with the provision of such services
4. Treatment of flat foot conditions and the prescription of supportive devices therefor
5. Treatment of subluxations of the foot, or routine foot care including the cutting or removal of corns or calluses, the trimming of nails, and other hygienic care. [P.L. 89-97 42 U.S.C. §1395y]

Such exclusions do not appear in federal statutes creating the Medicaid program, which provides federal funds to the states to assist them in caring for families and individuals in financial distress (42 U.S.C. §1396). That is not to say that the 50 states don't impose their own parsimonious limitations, but they are not so biased toward inpatient treatment in hospitals and against ambulatory care.

HOW MEDICARE CAME TO BE

"A page of history is worth a volume of logic," said Justice Holmes. Medicare was the first priority in President Lyndon Johnson's Great Society Program. It was envisaged at a time when one could still reasonably believe that everyone—old and young alike—was most sorely threatened by an acute "spell of illness," the expense of which could wipe a family out. And everyone believed medical miracles developed during and after World War II eventually could cure everything, even the normal signs of age. (Alvar Svanborg suggests in Chapter 2 that some professionals still so believe.)

Most of the support for Medicare for the elderly came from people who had long advocated and would have preferred universal sickness insurance, still an anathema to the medical establishment. If universal coverage supported by general taxation couldn't fly, care for the elderly supported by contributions to Social Security would at least be a start. Even so, the battle raged for two decades against the furious opposition of the American Medical Association. Not until Lyndon Johnson's overwhelming defeat of Barry Goldwater in the 1964 election did liberal Democrats have the votes to put it across.

The fight that culminated in the enactment of Medicare in 1965 began when most Americans saw hospitals at the center of the health universe with neighborhood clinics and relief stations as satellites, what one might call the pre–Copernican view of the health system. Financial barriers to access to the system's cures had to be surmounted, lest a "spell of illness" annihilate one's being or circumstances. The world changed while the fight raged. Drugs and innoculations conquered many fatal or disabling diseases. Palliatives and mechanical devices kept people ambulatory. But the Medicare fight was so bitter that its proponents dared not abandon the hospital focus nor add to its basic benefits. Those could come later, after the historic principle had been established.

The Medicare legislation was drafted by the House Ways and Means Committee, because it has jurisdiction over matters relating to Social Security and other taxes. The Ways and Means Committee writes the Internal Revenue Code and guards it very carefully. It is not surprising, therefore, that in drafting the Medicare statute, its staff, rather than empowering the Department of Health, Education and Welfare to establish by regulation programs that would provide health care to older Americans, surrounded it with statutory limits on eligibility that are now patrolled by a huge bureaucracy.

WHAT'S WRONG WITH MEDICARE?

Since its enactment 20 years ago, Medicare has reinforced medicine's domination of the health field and has become a major engine pushing elderly people into hospitals. Under Medicare, treatment, care, therapy, and paraphernalia normally provided for a particular diagnosis are reimbursable if a patient is confined to a hospital or proceeds to another institutional setting after a minimum hospital stay. Generally speaking, outpatient treatment, except for physician's services, is not reimbursable. As a consequence, providers tend to aggravate their estimate of patients' complaints, casting them as illnesses that can be cured in a hospital rather than as functional disorders that could be alleviated through supportive therapy at home or in some other less costly setting.

The tendency is financially enticing to patients, physicians, and hospitals, for the following reasons:

1. As explained earlier, patients cannot be reimbursed for care unless it is hospital connected. So older people needing care may choose to be hospitalized rather than pay for it as outpatients. Their families, with no other respite, support their choices.

2. Medicare reimburses doctors for each day a patient in their charge spends in a hospital. Doctors decide who needs hospitalization. The gatekeeper is paid to let people in.

3. Medicare payments for hospital care furnished to people over 65 increased from $5.94 billion in 1970 to $33.77 billion in 1981. The number of people over 65 discharged from hospitals increased from just under 6 million in 1971 to about 10.4 million in 1981, a rise of 74 percent. In the same period, the total number of people over 65 increased 43.6 percent.

The imbalance is explained partly by the fast-growing number of people over 75 who need more care. Also, treatments of special value to the elderly, such as hip replacement, bring more elderly to hospitals. At the same time, however, the reduction of pneumonia and heart disease has substantially reduced hospital admissions of older people. Speculation could go on, but, since the very old have become the fastest-growing segment in our population, we need to know much more about the real reasons for their hospitalization.

In the meantime, we do know that the decision to admit a patient to a hospital—always costly to patients and society at any age—is particularly significant for the elderly. They need reinforcement, stimulation, and challenge from their environment not institutional detachment from normal psychological supports, inducing dependency and depression. They are particularly vulnerable to overtreatment, since few physicians are trained to understand that there are many changes that accompany aging that are not pathological, as Alvar Svanborg points out in Chapter 2. When we mistake age with disease requiring hospitalization, not only the treasury, but also the body and the psyche are gravely damaged.

It is not simply in its incentive to hospitalize that the reimbursement system encourages diagnosis of complaints as pathological. Because reimbursement is not available until conditions warrant hospitalization, people allow their discomforts to ripen into disability before seeking care. Relatives often seek to be relieved of the burden of care; institutional care is subsidized while reimbursement for help in the home may be limited to a nurse's monthly visit to a blind diabetic.

Encouraging hospitalization is not the only perversity in Medicare. As pointed out earlier, Medicare prohibits reimbursement for various sorts of primary care, such as supportive devices for the feet, though everyone agrees that a health system should keep people ambulatory. And not only should they be able to walk around, they also need to function intelligently and adequately in society. But Medicare will not pay for routine physical checkups, eyeglasses, hearing aids, or immunizations.

So in Medicare we have developed a system that encourages institutionalization rather than independence, confinement instead of productivity, illness rather than health. In our endeavor to safeguard people against catastrophe, we have made commonplace the catastrophic conditions whose prevention we could afford.

WHAT CAN BE DONE TO IMPROVE MEDICARE?

There is a growing awareness that the financial prospects of Medicare are appalling. Predictions abound that the fund will be exhausted by 1990. A major change in focus away from hospitalization is mandatory. Instead, only tinkering or misguided adjustments in hospital cost control are proposed, for example, higher deductibles, disallowed tests, or lump sums for hospital treatment of particular maladies, so-called Diagnostic Related Groups (DRGs).

But the suggestion that reimbursement be extended for lower-cost treatment is opposed on the grounds that we cannot afford any add-ons that do not produce immediate savings. The greatest demonstrated savings result from keeping people out of hospitals. But beds aren't closed just because they are empty. Hospitals step up their efforts to bring in more patients through control of primary providers or instituting such new technology as transplants.

To break out of this vise, I think we must look at the problem a little more coherently and get beyond the semantic hang-up to which I referred to earlier: We speak of "health insurance," but most people aren't worried about protecting themselves from health; they worry about illness and its *medical* costs. They insure against casualty. People understand that they must pay for maintenance, either by fee for service or by service contract. With machines, prevention usually costs less than repair. There is some evidence that the same may be true with people.

As to the elderly, we are about to find out. A 1982 amendment to the Medicare statute (42 U.S.C. 1395mm) allows prepayment to health maintenance organizations (HMO's) or other organized care plans for beneficiaries who elect to subscribe. Regulations implementing the amendment were finally adopted in 1985. The recently completed Rand study of prepaid plans found that hospital usage was reduced by 28 percent for HMO members. Demonstration plans for the elderly are showing even more striking results: 60-percent reduction in hospitalization for elderly members of a prepaid plan in Worcester, Massachusetts. It is not only in cost savings, however, that such plans are useful to the elderly. Prepaid plans decide what benefits they will offer, without the statutory restrictions I discussed earlier.

Only through this device can appropriate health plans for the elderly be constructed. As Butler, Svanborg, and Birren declare in Chapters 1, 2, and 3 of this volume, the elderly are not simply older patients; their bodies behave differently from those of the young. What appears pathological may be normal. They respond differently to medication and may need close monitoring. They more often suffer from chronic conditions than they do "spells of illness" susceptible to cure through dramatic intervention. They need programs that are steadily supportive, not episodically invasive.

The following programs can be offered to elderly people whose membership in HMO is prepaid by Medicare:

1. *Health promotion.* Encourage people to exercise, control their weight and blood pressure, and supplement their diets. Preventive services should be available, including prophylactic dentistry, hearing and vision maintenance, routine foot care, physical therapy, and psychological counseling.
2. *Disease prevention.* Discourage smoking, obesity, abuse of alcohol, incoherent drug use, and isolation.
3. *Organized care.* Support multispecialty facilities where staff develop familiarity with the whole patient—prescribed medications; health; economic, social, and family status; housing

arrangements; group memberships; and so on. Referrals to specialists and institutions should be made on a deliberate rather than haphazard basis.

4. *Gatekeeping*. Admit patients to the least elaborate facility appropriate for their needs, where they can be followed by a local center that will arrange their return to the community.

Prepaid plans can encourage older people to continue in gainful activity, whether for monetary or psychological reward. Suggestions include:

1. Providing placement services in paid and voluntary employment and in educational institutions
2. Designing imaginative living arrangements, such as extended families of choice and congregate housing, as alternatives to isolation on the one hand and institutionalization on the other
3. Establishing day activity and care programs that enable the elderly to remain with their families or in noninstitutional living situations
4. Arranging local home-care services, such as meals and professional and social visits to the homebound, which defer institutionalization.

Services should be locally organized and coordinated and related to specialized facilities. They should be controlled by the elderly themselves, to assure that they are appropriate, provide gainful activity, and engage the elderly in the important decisions that affect their lives. That is to say, they should support what Jefferson interchangeably called "public happiness" or "public freedom" and what we at Salzburg called "productivity."

Through such devices the United States may yet allow its older citizens to seek the supportive care they need to remain independent and productive rather than be diminished to a condition where their only entitlement is to have hospitals and nursing homes reimbursed for their custodial care.

REFERENCES

Commerce Clearing House Medicare and Medicaid Guide ¶1406.
Commerce Clearing House Medicare and Medicaid Guide ¶1448.
Home Health Agency Manual HIM–11.

10

The United Nations World Assembly on Aging

Judith L. Howe

The United Nations sponsored a World Assembly on Aging in Vienna from July 26 to August 6, 1982, in order to focus attention at the regional, national, and international levels on the universal problem of aging. The original impetus for the assembly was provided by a resolution of the United States Congress in 1977. The proposal was transmitted to the United Nations, and in 1977 the General Assembly invited member states to submit their views on such a conference. In 1978 the United States, with strong support from Malta, obtained the approval of the General Assembly.

The World Assembly was the fifteenth special-topic global conference held by the United Nations since 1972. These global conferences have been convened to focus worldwide attention on a variety of topics with global implications, such as women and development, food, and population. Their purpose also has been to bring together, through the United Nations mechanism, member governments, with the hope of developing regional and international mechanisms and provoking governmental action in each nation.

Highlighting the problem of aging and its implications for the developing nations were principal reasons for convening the assembly. The demographic phenomenon of aging is more pronounced in the less-developed countries than in the developed nations. Whereas the developed nations will experience a 40-percent increase in their aged populations between the years 1975 and 2000, the developing world will experience a doubling, from 180 to 360 million persons aged 60 and over. This dramatic increase in the developing nations is largely the fruit of economic and social development and improvements in nutrition and health care.

THE PREPARATORY PROCESS

Convening the World Assembly on Aging involved an intricate preparatory process. Beginning in June, 1980, six regional technical meetings were held throughout the world, with four regional preparatory meetings following. Three of the four regional preparatory meetings focused on the views of less-developed countries (Economic and Social Commission for Asia and the Pacific, Economic Commission for Latin America, Economic Commission for Africa). Each of those three meetings generated a regional plan of action on aging, the prevalent theme of each plan being the central nature of the family unit and the negative impact that modernization, urbanization, and industrialization often have on traditional family structure. The fourth regional meeting, held by the Economic Commission for Europe, which I attended as a member of the United States delegation, essentially expressed the point of view of the developed countries. Recent experiences of European and North American nations have highlighted the demographic shift that less-developed countries are just beginning to confront. The action plan that emerged from the Economic Commission for Europe meeting reflects the various approaches that member governments have employed to meet the demands of a growing older population.

Simultaneous to these regional preparatory meetings were three meetings of the World Assembly's Advisory Committee, with representatives from 22 nations. The Advisory Committee was responsible for integrating and analyzing background materials generated by the technical and regional preparatory meetings, and for developing a draft international plan of action on aging for discussion and adoption at the assembly. Having represented the United States at both the second and third Advisory Committee meetings, I can attest that the plan was very carefully considered by the Advisory Committee members.

A meeting of sanctioned nongovernmental organizations was held in Vienna several months before the World Assembly, a significant event because nongovernmental organizations have never met prior to a World Assembly; they have only met concurrently. Holding such a forum before the World Assembly ensured that nongovernmental organizations had a formal advance plan for the assembly's consideration. In large part because of this different approach, nongovernmental organizations played a highly visible and active role at the assembly, with over 50 of them represented from throughout the world.

The preparation and submission of national reports were important opportunities for participation in the preparatory process for the assembly. While voluntary, approximately 70 nations developed such reports. Many of the national reports are comprehensive and arose from a process of identifying national issues and developing consensus.

THE INTERNATIONAL PLAN OF ACTION ON AGING

The World Assembly on Aging was organized into a plenary session and a simultaneous main committee meeting. In the plenary session, heads of delegations delivered remarks on behalf of their countries. Generally speaking, country representatives in the plenary session identified the family as the most important resource for providing care for the aged and considered institutionalization as the solution of last resort. Many representatives, however, did acknowledge in their statements that traditional family patterns and customs have been greatly eroded by industrialization and urbanization, with resulting strains on intergenerational relations and traditional family and community structures. There also was agreement in the plenary sessions that the growing disproportion in the distribution of sexes in older populations presents special challenges; in most nations, women are increasingly constituting a majority of the older population.

The substantive debate, however, was in the main committee, which was charged with reviewing the draft of the International Plan of Action on Aging. The negotiation process at any level is complex, but in an international setting it is exquisite. The draft plan of action was discussed paragraph by paragraph, and in some cases word by word, with each nation attempting to highlight its own particular concerns and perspectives. While the meeting generally was apolitical, cultural and societal diversities in definition and approach emerged during the debate.

Several principles underpin the International Plan of Action on Aging:

1. Development, both social and economic, should improve the well-being of all, on the basis of full participation in the process of development and the equitable distribution of derived benefits.
2. Individuals, regardless of age, sex, or creed, should contribute to the development process and receive benefits equitably.
3. Family unity is of major importance.
4. Voluntary organizations and volunteerism play a crucial role. Societies should be age-integrated with the elderly as full participants.
5. Governments, policy makers, and program administrators must consider aging as a natural phase of life.
6. Older persons themselves must be included in the development and implementation of all government policies, particularly those affecting them.

Since the World Assembly sought to highlight the implications of an aging population for the developing countries, a portion of the International Plan of Action on Aging concentrates on "development issues," which relate to the economic and resource characteristics of a society or region, such as levels of industrialization, migration patterns, income levels, the gross national product, and so on. Demographic factors, such as birth and death rates and life expectancy at birth, are determining factors as well, characterizing a country or region as either less developed or more developed. Despite the fact that at the beginning of the next century almost two-thirds of the world's aged will live in what are now considered to be developing or less-developed nations, governments in these countries are often so concerned with urgent, pressing problems of development that emerging issues, such as those related to aging, may be given short shrift.

The World Assembly's preparatory process appeared to be successful in meeting its goal of heightening attention on aging among the less-developed countries. In preparatory meetings and at the assembly itself, representatives from less-developed countries indicated that their nations are beginning to focus on age-related problems stemming from the development processes. For instance, in the Asian and Pacific regions, where 80 percent of the population is rural, the absence of social security or pension coverage was identified as a problem requiring action. In the Asian, Pacific, and Latin American regions, increased urbanization rates have resulted in a deterioration of traditional family and village life, and delegates reported that steps are being taken to intervene. In Africa, although aging has not yet been identified as a high-priority issue because of the relatively small percentage of aged at this time, concerns for the aged population and demographic trends are being taken into greater account in future development planning. As in the other developing regions, deterioration of the traditional extended family structure and its impact on the care of the aged is a central concern in Africa.

The International Plan of Action on Aging addresses six areas of concern to aging individuals, referred to as the "humanitarian issues": (1) health and nutrition, (2) income security and employment, (3) housing and environment, (4) family, (5) social welfare, and (6) education. These are concerns for people of all ages, but take on increasing importance with age and become increasingly interdependent with advancing years.

Health and Nutrition

Clearly, one of the most pressing issues facing all nations of the world, both developed and less developed, is the provision of adequate and humane health care to their aged populations. Contrary to the belief of many, the vast majority of aged are independent and need minimal support, particularly in the developed world. In the United States, for instance, just 6 percent of the population aged 65 and over is institutionalized. In all societies, the greatest demand on health care services is among the "old old," those 80 years and over. In fact, this is the most rapidly growing age group in most regions of the world, particularly in the developing nations.

The International Plan of Action on Aging highlights the special needs of the "old old," recognizing their particular vulnerabilities, and suggests that their needs are met best through a primary care approach. In addition to focusing on the importance of primary care for the aged, the plan of action sets forth a number of other recommendations in the area of health care, including the need for closer coordination between social welfare and health services, the importance of education in self-care and health promotion, and the principle that older people should participate in decisions regarding their health care.

Income Security and Employment

Income security refers to the guarantee, as a matter of public policy, of sufficient income to support minimal standards of living. The plan of action focuses on the need for universal coverage throughout the world, emphasizing the special situation of older women, whose income is generally lower than that of men and whose employment often has been broken by maternal and family responsibilities. The issue of age discrimination in employment was addressed as well; it was recommended that older people be assisted in finding new employment opportunities through training and retraining programs. For instance, small-scale village industries in the less-developed countries should be reactivated, with participation geared toward the aged. Other recommendations called for flexible work programs for older workers and aids in the workplace that are designed to allow those who are more frail to continue working.

Housing and Environment

Housing is an issue of particular importance to the aged, since their homes are often the center of all daily activities. The plan of action stresses the importance of the social and psychological aspects of housing and calls for coordination of housing services with other community services. The plan also recommends that older people be assisted in remaining in their homes for as long as possible through various measures, such as home-adaptation programs.

Family

The plan recommends strengthening the family role in caring for the aged, through a number of specific measures, including increased home health care programs, financial incentives to families for the care of the aged, respite programs and day hospitals that relieve families caring for the sick aged, and design of housing that is conducive to multigenerational living.

Social Welfare

Only in the last 40 to 50 years have specialized social welfare services for the aged been organized, and generally this has been done only in the developed countries. Therefore, throughout most of the world, older persons are unserved by social welfare programs. The plan of action calls for the development of a continuum of social services, coordinated by governmental and nongovernmental organizations, interfaced with health, housing, and other community services and programs.

Education

In many cases, rapid social change has resulted in information obsolescence and, consequently, social obsolescence for older people. The plan of action calls for a lifelong educational approach, with access to educational programs as well as provision of opportunities for the aged to serve as transmitters of knowledge and culture to the young. The plan also recommends the development of media and educational efforts aimed at dissolving stereotypes about the aged and the aging process and presenting a realistic and positive view of aging.

IMPLEMENTING THE PLAN

The International Plan of Action on Aging acknowledges that its success depends largely on actions undertaken by member governments. First, it recommends that governments take measures to highlight the issue of aging and that they take advantage of resources offered by intergovernmental, nongovernmental, and aging organizations. Specifically, the plan designates the Economic and Social Council of the 36-nation Commission on Social Development as the United Nations body responsible for reviewing implementation of the plan on a four-year cycle.

Second, the plan designates the United Nations Center for Social Development and Humanitarian Affairs as a focal point for plan follow-up; it also recommends that the center be strengthened in terms of staff support and resources.

Third, the plan recommends the continuance of the World Assembly on Aging Trust Fund, designed to provide technical assistance to developing countries, to which governments and private organizations may contribute. Many governments have contributed to the fund; the United States contributed $650,000, the world's largest contributor.

Finally, the plan suggests that mechanisms be established and strengthened that will promote technical support and cooperation, and that activities be undertaken that will promote the exchange of information and experiences at the international level.

Although the United States played an active role in the World Assembly on Aging preparatory activities and at the assembly itself, there has been little follow-up here. There has been some follow-up in other countries, however. France, for example, convened a national conference of older persons in March 1983, to address the issues raised by the assembly and to discuss means of implementing the recommendations at the national level. President Mitterand has committed France to the creation of an international information center on aging, to facilitate the exchange of knowledge. In the fall of 1983, Canada also held a follow-up conference, as have the Nordic countries.

The plan recommends periodic assessment of World Assembly follow-up activities at the national level. The response of the United States government has been disappointing. While a nongovernmental organization, the American Association of International Aging, has been established with seed monies from private foundations, in order to follow through the World Assembly's recommendations, a coordinated governmental response is needed to demonstrate an American commitment to the aged and the concept of global conferences.

Postscript

Betty Friedan

Dealing with age and health in terms of productivity has forced us to reject excessively masculine definitions of productivity and, instead, to bring into our very definitions of productivity some qualities of human sensitivity and human need that in the United States, at least, have been relegated to the female.

This integration happened at Salzburg. While I have drawn many analogies to the women's movement because it provides some sense of how things change when we come to terms with personhood, I would not close with the idea that I think the age question and the woman question are identical. As far as I know from my study of the state of the art in America, the seminar in Salzburg was the first conference on age that started to deal with aging, not in terms of the care of the infirm, the pathological, the deteriorating, or even the terminal aging that all of us will ultimately experience, but in terms of health and productivity. It forced us to deal with old people in society, just as dealing with the question of sex discrimination in employment forced us to confront the personhood of women.

In the next 20 years, both in the developed nations and in less-developed nations, dramatic demographic changes are going to focus more and more attention on new values, new possibilities, and new problems that come with the aging of all nations, as well as on the new promise of these years. There will have to be some confrontational political movement centered on age, but somehow I don't see single-issue politics as the answer here. When we ask for restructuring of employment and more flexible possibilities for employment, we can't do it in terms of the aged alone. There will have to be coalitions to make it happen, coalitions of unions, business, women, and others.

Such restructuring will have to be for everyone. I don't conceive of a battle of old against young, not in the way the women's movement, unfortunately, sometimes seemed to be women against men. Yet there will have to be confrontation with age discrimination wherever it exists, and it will take wisdom to make the necessary coalitions.

We have talked about the need to find new ways of housing and new ways of meeting the needs for intimacy of the aged. We have talked about productivity, giving employers incentives to make new use of the special values and wisdom of older people. We have talked about the importance of research to delineate what those really are.

Innovations of which we cannot now even conceive will come in the next 20 years. As age consciousness becomes widespread, innovations will appear in lifestyles, concepts, values, and songs, just as they did from young people 20 years ago, just as they did from women 10 years ago. Demographic pressures will give rise to these innovations, but they will be shaped by the elderly, using the wisdom that comes with age itself.

Welcome to age!

Appendix A

Process and Perception: The Flavor and Framework of the Salzburg Seminar on Health, Productivity, and Aging

Mal Schechter

At the Salzburg Seminar on Health, Productivity, and Aging, 32 Fellows from 15 countries found "productivity" the center of gravity in the triad of the title and quickly established in their own minds the close relationship between the health of the elderly and their productivity and, conversely, the relationship of illness to inactivity.

Certain institutional arrangements work to dismiss or trivialize the actual and potential productivity of older people. Given the dramatic demographic trends in many lands toward rapidly rising populations of older people, particularly at the ages in which illness and disability rates are high, the seeming willingness of society to discard this potential productivity should be termed misguided, at best.

The Fellows at Salzburg found that they had to test their own perceptions about aging, health, and productivity before undertaking the emerging task of constructing principles for new attitudes and actions. The process produced three reports of different character from the varied cultural, geographic, and personal backgrounds of the participants. Yet these varied reports contained many convergences as well as divergences of thought.

Perhaps some key themes relative to action were captured best by the group under Dr. James Birren of the United States, in their statement calling on us to:

1. Foster the participation of older persons in all spheres of society
2. Find a balance between dependence and efforts to achieve independence for older persons
3. Learn from regional, cultural, economic, social, historical, demographic, and political diversity
4. Recognize individuation with age
5. View aging as a lifelong process of change
6. Understand older persons' needs for connection with others through interpersonal and intimate relations
7. Modify societal attitudes toward the elderly and the aging process.

Another common theme was inclusion. The study group under Dr. Alvar Svanborg of Sweden concluded that it is essential to eliminate the explicit and tacit exclusions encountered by older people in many societies.

Similarly, the group led by Betty Friedan of the United States declared that "the elderly must be significantly and responsibly included in every aspect of policy formulation, implementation, and evaluation."

In a colloquy after drafts of the study group papers were heard, Dr. Nacer Chraibi of Morocco, moderating a final session of the seminar, seemed to speak for many of the Fellows when he identified a process and a bedrock issue:

> All of us have been changed in this seminar. Let me explain how consciousness changes us. In a coronary care unit, I find patients aged 30 to 50 with arrhythmias. Modern techniques of care do not deal with all of a patient's needs. For example, a patient asked me one day whether his heart problem would affect his sexual activity in the future. I explained that his life would be normal in this respect. Later, I took it on myself *not to wait* for patients to ask such important questions.
>
> So I tell you that, if you can identify with people, you can understand and prevent problems from worsening. And this empathy will change ideas. I did not think much about aging before coming here. I have learned, however, that there is no aging issue. There is only a human issue. When we put aside our selfish perspectives and stop assigning responsibility to other people, then the issue becomes ours.

A degree of modesty proceeding from awareness of their limitations characterized the Fellows' discussions and accounted, in part, for acknowledgement of particular needs for research. It was not clear, for example, to what degree older people were willing and able in different societies to work at paid or unpaid employment. Likewise, many Fellows saw their explorations as just touching the tip of the iceberg.

For this reason, the Fellows were unprepared to label their work as much more than a guide to action or principles. One Fellow, Dr. Anna Howe of Australia, objected to the many "shoulds" in the reports she heard. "It's easy to say 'should.' 'Could' is harder." She preferred recommendations for priorities of action. She urged consideration of how the elderly could get a better hold on resources.

Dr. Svanborg said he agreed with Dr. Howe totally on the eventual need to convert principles into priorities for action. However, as he saw it, the work of the study group was to concentrate on identifying problems the Fellows thought they might be able to do something about. At the same time, he continued, it was impossible to work out concrete implementations, since the Fellows came from many lands.

Concurring, Uri Laor of Israel commented that it would be presumptuous for the Fellows to decide what priorities different societies should choose. In one country it might be education; in another it might be home care. No, he said, the Fellows should stick to the identification of principles that would lend themselves to implementation in various contexts of culture and nationality.

One key issue for women was not reflected in the reports, commented Linda Berglin, a state senator from Minnesota: The problem of poverty is greater for widowed or single women than for men, and the factors that worsen their poverty are not changing dramatically. She urged special priority be given to this issue, and many Fellows agreed.

Dr. Graham Rowles of the United States made a plea that the association of aging, productivity, and health should not blind the Fellows to an implicit theme: Productivity of any sort is based on survival. "Many older people," said Rowles, "have not achieved the basic ability to survive. It is important to state that all older people should be able to survive."

Dr. Chraibi immediately added his view that "if you survive to 65, you have done enough and have been productive enough and should be supported. That's achievement enough. Productivity may be the wrong idea if we use it to justify life. Why should anyone have to justify life in terms of productivity?"

Barriers to recognizing the potentials of later life include ignorance, negative attitudes, and institutionalization of agism, or prejudice against the elderly, according to Dr. Gary Andrews of Australia. To demonstrate how the identification of barriers might lead to implementation strategies, Dr. Andrews went to a blackboard and drew a matrix (see Table A.1) with categories for target groups, strategies, media for reaching the target, objectives, and goals. As the table demonstrates, this was an enlightening exercise and left us with a clearer picture of how to turn thought into action.

While discussion of the Fellows might be summed up in various ways, a consistent theme—the individual's quest for consciousness—recurred often enough to be counted as a dominant one. Dr. Birren suggested that Dr. Andrews' chart be developed to cover forces inside as well as outside the individual. He asked the Fellows to think about what ideas of theirs were changed as a result of the seminar; this challenge was picked up immediately and became the final day's agenda.

For the larger future, the Fellows seemed to have their own action plans. Consciousness was bearing fruit. The process was plain to Ms. Friedan, known for her leadership in the women's movement. She noted how she herself and others had developed new sensitivities in their work over the previous two weeks. "In my seminar in the last few days I heard people saying, 'When I go home, there is this issue or that problem I will look at. We are trying to identify the themes. We have no inherent power but as individuals we can work to get action in our own countries.' "

TABLE A.1. Matrix prepared by Dr. Gary Andrews

Barriers	Target Group	Strategy	Medium	Objectives	Goals
Ignorance	Community, middle aged professionals, decision makers	Research, dissemination of knowledge, and training	Professional literature, mass media	Specific, time-related research: lab, clinical, epidemiological	To understand the aging process and its consequences fully
Negative Attitudes	Community, aged incl. professionals, employees	Education and publicity	Educational process: public, private, child, adult, and vocational training	Specific changes in attitude among key groups	To achieve a positive and rational acceptance of aging and view the aged as adult contributors
Institution-alization of agism: legal, educational, occupational, economic, governmental (public policy)	Community, legislators, decision makers, special lobby groups	Political action, propaganda and affirmative action	Political and institutional process	Specific, time-related removal of discrimination in key areas and achievement of participation	To achieve the integration of the aged into society with full rights and privileges in all regards

Appendix B

Statement of Common Themes and Principles on Health, Productivity, and Aging Developed by the Participants in Plenary and Seminar Sessions

In general, older persons are an integral part of society and aging is a lifelong process. As stated in the Plan of Action of the United Nations 1982 World Assembly on Aging, "Aging, in addition to being a symbol of experience and wisdom, can also bring human beings closer to personal fulfillment, according to their beliefs and aspirations." All policies and programs geared toward the aged should maximize the highest human potential of each individual, acknowledging lifelong changes with age and affirming the emergence of certain unique qualities that can enhance productivity. The elderly must be significantly and responsibly involved in every effort to achieve this goal.

COMMON THEMES

1. Older persons should participate in all spheres of society.
2. A balance must be maintained between dependence and independence for older persons.
3. Regional, cultural, economic, social, historical, demographic, and political diversity require recognition.

4. Individuation with age should be appreciated.

5. Aging is a lifelong process of change.

6. Older persons need connection with others through interpersonal and intimate relations.

7. Societal attitudes toward the elderly and the aging process must be modified.

8. Age-specific policies, fair as they may appear, can reinforce stereotypes and segregate the elderly from the mainstream of society.

9. Age-specific policies may be more politically attractive than other approaches in societies where the elderly have been recognized as being strikingly disadvantaged.

10. The elderly can be defined as a group for policy making on the basis of needs specific to them, as in the case of geriatric medicine and long-term care.

PRINCIPLES

Health and Productivity

1. Health care should enable people to function to the limit of their physical, psychological, and social capacities. Therefore, care that emphasizes health promotion, disease prevention, and integration of services is preferred over institutionalization. Any services that induce dependency should be discouraged.

2. Productive participation in society is essential to health.

3. Smoking and abuse of alcohol and drugs appear to accelerate aging and induce disease and should be discouraged in every way.

4. Health care policy should encourage every older person to keep active outside institutions.

Employment and Productivity

1. All laws and arrangements with respect to work, retirement, and pensions which discriminate on the basis of age and sex should be re-examined and phased out where inappropriate.

2. *sole* Employment policies offering the widest possible range of options for all persons to contribute to the productivity of the community, region, or nation will promote both individual self-esteem and enhance social and economic development. Such policies will enable individuals to vary their work hours, schedules, locations, and time involvement in accordance with changing personal abilities and needs and societal requirements for productivity.

3. Programs should be established for retraining employees, adapting places and conditions of work to the abilities of the elderly, and counseling people for paid and volunteer employment.

4. Employers should be given incentives and advice that will encourage them to use the special skills and wisdom of the elderly.

5. The experience and skills of older people are valuable assets of any community, and the trends in developed countries to reduce their participation in the labor force should be monitored closely and examined for causal factors. Planning efforts should be undertaken to devise methods of stabilizing if not reversing the trends toward decreasing labor-force participation of older people. In particular, the effects of pension plans and their accumulating burden of indebtedness on the productivity of societies should be studied.

6. Jobs should be redesigned to accommodate older workers, providing for mobility within an organization by removing age barriers to retraining and transfer and offering in-service training, flexible work arrangements, and phased retirement.

7. No portion of a nation's job pool should be specifically reserved for the elderly; chronological age is not a useful criterion for job assignment. Allocation by age reinforces intergenerational divisiveness, and retirement income systems can be weakened.

Productivity Equivalents

1. When they are independent, creative, and contributing to society, the elderly confer economic and social benefits that

must be counted as productivity and that society must acknowledge and reward.

2. In addition to their ongoing contributions within the economic system, the elderly can bring to society unique qualities that accrue from their lifelong experience and the process of having aged. Societies should utilize this experience and wisdom in ways that are meaningful both to the elderly and the communities in which they live. Such opportunities might include child care and education, peer group assistance, and political action.

3. Persons of all ages should have effective access to the resources of society and participate equally in the sociopolitical activities aimed at attaining equity in terms of effective representation and access to available resources.

4. Older people should be encouraged to participate in political activities aimed at attaining equity in access to available resources.

Education

1. Education should prepare people from childhood to be aware of longer life and the psychological and social aspects of aging and its benefits and limitations.

2. Medical schools and other professional schools, such as social work, dentistry, nursing, psychology, architecture, journalism, and divinity, should include material in their curricula on the processes of aging and on the services required by older persons.

3. Systematic studies should be made of the curricula of institutions of higher education with regard to the inclusion of the subject matter of aging and the life circumstances of older persons. In addition, surveys should be made of the content and extent of research on aging. Networks of information exchange for research information on aging should be established within nations and between nations.

4. The curricula of all professions—architecture, medicine, teaching, religion—should be gerontized so that they provide facilities and programs attractive and accessible to older people.

5. People currently serving the elderly—physicians, bus

drivers, priests, teachers, government officials, retail clerks, family members—should be acquainted with the facts of aging and the appropriate response thereto.

6. Educational opportunities should be available throughout the life cycle, with emphasis on self-development, training, and integration of older people into society.

7. Educational programs should be instituted for journalists, planners, and others in executive and communicative positions, about the productive capacities and needs of the elderly.

8. The elderly should be taught how to improve their health, prevent disease, care for themselves, make financial decisions, use services, nourish themselves properly, and avoid overmedication.

9. All patronizing programs that treat the elderly as children should be discontinued.

Attitudes

1. The growing number of elderly eventually can change political, market, and media incentives.

2. Society must accord full rights to the elderly and expect them to discharge their share of responsibility.

3. Steps should be taken to break through the mystique of age and establish images in the minds of relevant professionals, policy makers, the public, and the elderly themselves, showing the elderly as productive participants in society and delineating their special skills.

4. Independence is to be encouraged, but dependence is not necessarily pathological. Interdependency among generations and family members should be viewed as a positive and normal status. Traditional societies' structures and religious teaching support this concept.

5. All individuals, for reasons of illness, environmental or psychological stress, or life circumstances, from time to time will need more support. Periods of enforced dependency should be viewed as transitional, with the goal that, where possible and with appropriate assistance, a person can overcome disability and regain optimal functioning.

6. Individuals have a right to expect that changing societal values will not jeopardize the economic and social credits that they may have accumulated previously.

7. An individual's productive contribution should be considered over an extended period of time.

8. Trade unions should be aware of the productivity of older people and prepare preretirement programs for those who want or need to retire.

9. Older people must organize themselves as a pressure group in order to fight discrimination.

Research

1. More knowledge should be collected on the innovative capacity of older workers, which they have derived from experience and wisdom.

2. Demographic changes create a need for increasingly sophisticated information about the processes of aging. Research of a basic and applied character is needed to provide knowledge for effective services to the aged and for planning, implementing, and evaluating services.

3. Longitudinal research studies are needed, to determine the trends in the population with regard to a wide range of aspects of aging, such as age-specific incidence and prevalence of disease, extent of disability, social and economic resources of older persons, loneliness, mental health, adaptive capacities, and skills.

4. Efforts are needed that encourage the use of research so that new knowledge can enhance the quality of life for older adults.

5. Biological, psychological, and social research is needed that identifies the processes of aging and develops interventions for reducing disability and excessive dependency and encourages productive roles for older persons.

6. Research should be promoted among theologians and social scientists on the spirituality of older people, particularly its flow with age.

7. Patterns of aging are different for men than for women. Women live longer, often alone and poor. Such differences

must be understood and policies shaped to accommodate them. Research should explore how to lengthen life for men.

Environment

1. Barriers to the elderly in the environment should be identified and eliminated.
2. Housing policy should allow the elderly to remain in their homes, encourage heterogeneous communities, and provide for extended families of choice.
3. All community facilities should be open to the elderly for use and employment. Personnel responsible for running them should be instructed in creating arrangements and adaptations that make these facilities accessible to the elderly.
4. Transportation systems should eliminate barriers, such as steps on buses that are too high and traffic signals that do not allow enough time for older pedestrians. Integration of special transportation with general transportation should be considered. (The issue of elderly people driving automobiles was not resolved.)

Independence

1. Institutionalization should be deferred for as long as possible and family members should be included in the development of plans for medical and social care. Care givers should be supported with respite services. An individual's privacy, including opportunity for sexual activity, should be preserved to the greatest degree possible in group living arrangements.
2. All people, including the elderly, have the right to make decisions about their lives, including decisions about care. Interference or suppression of this right and responsibility deprives individuals of a sense of control over their lives, a deprivation that has negative consequences to health and productivity.
3. Many older people, both men and women, are still without the necessary means for "survival." Emphasis on productivity should not distract us from the fundamental goal of providing basic economic support to disadvantaged elderly.

Appendix C

Health and Pension Systems for the Elderly, Selected Countries

Helena Pontes Carreira

Countries	Retirement Age		Type	Universal	Pension system	
	Males	Females			Type	Universal
1 Australia	65 (4)	60 (4)	Dual: Universal and Social Assistance System (S.A.S.) (2)	Yes (v.(2))	Cash Benefits: S.A.S. (3) Medical Benefits: Dual S.A.S. and S.I.S. (4)	—
2 Egypt	60 (5)	60 (5)	Social Insurance System (S.I.S.)	—	S.I.S. (6)	—
3 Greece	65 (7)	60 (7)	Social Insurance System (S.I.S.)	—	S.I.S. (8)	—
4 Hungary	60	55	Social Insurance System (S.I.S.)	—	Dual: S.I.S. (Cash ben.) and Universal (moderate care) (9)	Yes (Medical Care)
5 Israel	65 (10)	60 (11)	Social Insurance System (S.I.S.)	—	S.I.S. (Cash maternity benefits only) (11)	—
6 Jordan	60	55 (12)	Social Insurance System (S.I.S.)	—	(13)	—
7 Morocco	60 (14)	60 (14)	Social Insurance System (S.I.S.)	—	S.I.S. (Cash benefits only) (15)	—

#	Country			Pension System		Benefits	
8	Netherlands	65 (16)	65 (16)	Social Insurance System (S.I.S.)	Yes (17)	S.I.S. (Separate but Interlocking programs of cash and medical benefits) (18)	Yes
9	N. Ireland	65 (20)	60 (20)	Dual: S.I.S. and S.A.S.	Yes (21)	Dual: Insurance (Cash Benefits) and M.H.S. (22)	Yes (23)
10	Poland	65 (24)	60 (24)	Social Insurance System (S.I.S.)	—	S.I.S. (Cash and medical benefits) (25)	—
11	Portugal	65 (26)	62 (26)	Social Insurance System (S.I.S.)	—	S.I.S. (Cash and medical benefits) (27)	—
12	Spain	65 (28)	65 (28)	Social Insurance System (S.I.S.)	—	S.I.S. (Cash and medical benefits) (29)	—
13	Sweden	65 (30)	65 (30)	Dual: Universal Pension and S.I.S. (30)	Yes	S.I.S. (Cash and medical benefits) (31)	Yes
14	United States	65	65 (32)	Social Insurance System (S.I.S.)	—	S.I.S. (33)	—

Source: Social Community Programs Throughout the World: 198⁻

NOTES TO HEALTH AND PENSION SYSTEMS TABLE

1   (1)   Old-age pension; disability pension; age 16 or over, loss of 85% of working capacity; or blindness.

      (2)   Old-age: 10 years of continuous residence (5 years with total residence of 15); income-tested, unless age 70. Disability pension: permanent residence and limited income, unless claimant blind.

      (3)   Income-tested, adjusted in May and November according to price changes.

      (4)   Hospital benefits: Free care in shared room and treatment by doctors engaged by the hospital for uninsured persons; free choice of doctor and accommodation by privately insured.

2   (5)   Old-age pension with 120 months of contribution (or age 55 with 240 months of contribution).

      (6)   Sickness benefits: 75% daily wage during first 90 days of sickness.
Medical benefits: Includes general and specialist care, surgery, hospitalization, maternity care, dental care, laboratory services, medicines, appliances, and transportation.

3   (7)   Old-age pension with 4050 days of contribution; age 60 (men) and 55 (women) with 3240 of 4050 days in arduous or unhealthy employment.

      (8)   Sickness benefits: 50% of earnings, according to 22 wage classes, plus 10% of benefit for each dependent. Medical benefits: includes general and specialist care; care in hospital, sanatorium, or nursing home; medicine; maternity care; dental care; appliances; and transportation.

4   (9)   Cash benefits (SIS): 65% of earnings or 75% if 2 years of continuous employment.
Medical benefits universal: Includes general and specialist care, hospitalization, sanatorium, dental care, maternity care, medicines, and travel expenses.

5 (10)   Old-age pension: 5 years of insurance in last 10 or 12 years' total insurance (no qualifying period for insured women,

divorced, deserted, married to uninsured husband, or un-
married and aged 55 or over at time of immigration).

(11)   Sickness benefit: None under insurance.
Maternity benefit: 75% of earnings, adjusted for cost-of-liv-
ing.
Medical benefits: None under national insurance program
(most workers insured for medical care with voluntary sickness fund).

6   (12)   Old-age pension: With 120 months continuous coverage (36
months within last 5 years), or 15 years intermittent coverage.

(13)   There is only a special sickness insurance system for public
employees. (Medical services available to population in
government clinics and hospitals within limit of facilities
available).

7   (14)   Old-age pension at 55 for miners with 5 years or more of
underground work (employees and apprentices in industry,
commerce, cooperatives, and liberal professions).

(15)   Sickness benefit: 50% of covered earnings up to 26 weeks.
Medical benefits: None provided.

8   (16)   Old-age pension if contributions paid each year from age 15
through 64; otherwise reduced pension.

(17)   All residents (old age and survivor pension); all residents
over 18 (disability pension).

(18)   Sickness benefit: 80% of earnings up to a certain daily maximum.
Maternity benefit: 100% of earnings.
Medical benefits: General and specialist care, hospitalization, laboratory services, medicine, limited dental care,
maternity care, appliances, rehabilitation, and transportation.

(19)   Medical benefits: Compulsory coverage for wage earners
and salaried employees; voluntary coverage for other persons (mainly self-employed) and pensioners with income
below certain amount.
Cash benefits: All wage earners and salaried employees.

9 (20) Old-age pension if 50 weeks of paid contributions before April 1978 or 52 weeks of paid contributions for any one year after April 1978.

(21) All residents.

(22) Sickness benefit: Flat benefit of £20.65 a week, £12.75 for wife or dependent, £1.25 for each child.

Medical benefit: Includes general practitioner care, specialist services, hospitalization, maternity care, dental care, medicine, appliances, home nursing, and family planning.

(23) Cash sickness and maternity benefits: Employed persons. Medical care: All residents.

10 (24) Old-age pension after 20 years (men) and 15 years (women) employment; covers employees, apprentices, collective farmers, members of cooperatives for artisans, etc. Special systems for miners, railroad employees, police, and independent farmers.

(25) Sickness benefit: 100% of earnings average over preceding 13 weeks, if 8 years of employment (80% if 3 to 8 years, 75% if less than 3).

Maternity benefit: 100% of earnings.

Medical benefits: Includes general and specialist care; care in hospital or sanatorium; 70% of cost of medicine; dental care; and maternity care by midwife or doctor, at home or in hospital.

11 (26) Old-age pension at age 60 if unemployed 720 days, at age 70 if retired from insured employment. Covers employees in industry, commerce and services, wage and salary earners in agricultural enterprises, domestic servants, and self-employed. Special systems for fishermen, seamen, farm laborers, some liberal professions, railway employees, and rural workers.

Social pensions: Anyone not covered under contributory pension programs.

(27) Sickness benefit: 60% of earnings (80% to 100% if tuberculosis).

Maternity benefit: 100% of earnings payable for up to 90 days.

Medical benefits: General and specialist care; hospitalization; maternity care; surgery; and listed medicines.

12 (28) Old-age pension at age 65 (lower for difficult, dangerous, or unhealthy work), 10 years of contribution including 700 days of contribution in last 7 years; civil servants at age 70. Coverage: Employees in industry and services (classified according to 12 occupational classes). Special systems for agricultural workers, domestic servants, railway employees, salesmen, self-employed, seamen, public employees, miners, and liberal professions.

(29) Sickness benefit: 60% of covered earnings.
Maternity benefit: 75% of covered earnings.
Medical benefits: Includes general and specialist care, hospitalization, medicine, dental care, maternity care, laboratory services, appliances, and transportation.

13 (30) Old-age pension at age 65 (60–64 with .5% reduction per month, or full pension if unable to cope with job or if unemployed with no prospect of job). Covers all resident citizens and aliens who have fulfilled stipulated periods of residence. Earnings-related pension for all employees and self-employed persons earning over "base amount."

(31) Sickness benefit: 90% of income up to 7½ times base amount.
Medical benefits: Doctor's consultation, patient pays 25 kronor per visit (30 kronor to private doctor). Free hospitalization in ward or public hospital; free medicine up to 40 kronor per purchase; cost of confinement, including care in maternity ward; refund of part of travel cost; dental care (patient pays ½ of cost), and specified appliances. Covers all residents.

14 (32) Old-age pension at age 65 (62–64 with reduction). Covers gainfully occupied persons, including self-employed. Excludes casual agricultural and domestic employment, and limited self-employment.

(33) Sickness benefit: 50% of earnings, variable by states.
Maternity benefit: Variable.

Medical benefits: Services furnished by providers paid directly by carriers or refunds to patients by carriers of part of medical expenses. Hospitalization: 90 days in-patient care for each illness plus 60 days lifetime reserve; posthospital skilled nursing facility care for additional 100 days; laboratory and X-ray services for in-patient; and posthospital home health services. Covers hospitalization of all insured workers or pensioners age 65 or over, certain others who qualify at age 65, disability pensioners on rolls for more than 2 years; and persons with chronic kidney disease. Special national systems for railroad employees (cash benefits), and federal, state system for medically indigent (Medicaid).

Appendix D

A Perspective
on Social Involvement
(Social Vitality?)

John McCallum

Types of Social Organizations:

1. **Social "Life" Worlds**—e.g., collecting stamps, art and music appreciation, traditional interests
2. **Community and Informal Groups**—e.g., neighborhood, some clubs
3. **Voluntary Association**—normally providing welfare services
4. **Interest Groups**—organizing for a political party, or for a single issue (e.g., nuclear disarmament)
5. **Religious Affiliations**—appreciation of god(s), immanent and/ or transcendent, alone or organized
6. **Formal Work Organizations**—labor is exchanged for income, measurable output; diffuse or centralized organization

Within social organizations there is a typical hierarchy of social functions:

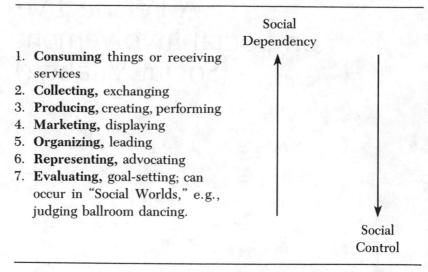

1. **Consuming** things or receiving services
2. **Collecting,** exchanging
3. **Producing,** creating, performing
4. **Marketing,** displaying
5. **Organizing,** leading
6. **Representing,** advocating
7. **Evaluating,** goal-setting; can occur in "Social Worlds," e.g., judging ballroom dancing.

Social Dependency

Social Control

Note: Similar models can be found in D. Unruh, *Invisible Lives* (Sage, 1983) and other authors.

Organizational productivity (output per unit of input) and individual job performance (rate of performance of specified task) are appropriate and central questions for some interest groups, voluntary associations, and formal work organizations.

In "modernized" societies the importance and satisfaction involved with *social life worlds* is often neglected.

Index